M. Allen Cunningham

We Are Guests of Ancient Time

Essays & Variations
on the
Imagination,
Memory, Seeing,
and Media

ATELIER26 BOOKS : Samizdat Series vol. 4
Portland, Oregon

We Are Guests of Ancient Time: Essays & Variations on the
Imagination, Memory, Seeing, and Media (Nonfiction)

isbn-13: 978-1-7329896-8-9
Library of Congress Control Number: 2023942371
Atelier26 Books: *Samizdat Series* Vol. 4

Atelier26 Books are printed in the U.S.A. on acid-free paper.

Cover design by Nathan Shields
Interior design by M.A.C.

ATELIER26 BOOKS, an independent press in
Portland, OR, exists to demonstrate the powers
and possibilities of literature through beautifully
designed and expressive books that get people
talking, listening, and exchanging ideas. Our
books have been honored by the PEN/Hemingway Award, the
PEN/Robert W. Bingham Prize, the Balcones Fiction Prize,
and the Flann O'Brien Award, and cited on numerous Best of
the Year lists. Visit Atelier26Books.com

The valued support of Jason Headley helped make this book
possible.

 This book was funded in part by the
Regional Arts & Culture Council.

M. Allen Cunningham

We Are Guests of Ancient Time

M. ALLEN CUNNINGHAM published his debut novel *The Green Age of Asher Witherow* at age twenty-six. That novel was selected by the American Booksellers Association as a #1 Indie Next Pick, was a finalist for the Indie Next Book of the Year Award with Marilynne Robinson's *Gilead* and Philip Roth's *The Plot Against America*, and was listed among the "Best Books of the West" in the *Salt Lake Tribune*. Three years later, Cunningham released *Lost Son*, a large biographical novel about Rainer Maria Rilke which was the culmination of more than ten years of reading, writing, research, and travel. Distinguished literary critic Ihab Hassan said "the magic of Rilke reach[es] out from every page." *Lost Son* was added to Europe's official Rilke bibliography and was listed as a Top Ten Book in *The Oregonian*. Cunningham has subsequently published seven other books, most recently *Q&A*, a novel inspired by the 1950s American quiz show scandals. His novel *Partisans* was a Flann O'Brien Award finalist, and *The Honorable Obscurity Handbook*, his existential guide to the creative life, was lauded by Cynthia Ozick as "ingenious, important, wholly absorbing, inspiring and inspiriting." Cunningham's short story collection *Date of Disappearance* has appeared in illustrated limited edition from Atelier26 Books. *The Flickering Page*, Cunningham's treatise on the socio-cultural and political implications of electronic text, weaves together some of the most cogent thought about technology and technological revolutions from the past fifty years, and features original illustrations by Nathan Shields. Over the past twenty years Cunningham's essays and stories have appeared in many distinguished publications. He is the recipient of several grants and fellowships, as well as residencies at the Yaddo Colony. An educator and frequent public speaker, he teaches creative writing courses for undergraduates and composition and film courses for accelerated high school students.

For my family — here, before, and beyond

VARIATION IS PERHAPS THE MOST "OPEN" of musical procedures, one which gives the greatest freedom to the composer's fantasy. It mirrors the unpredictability and chance nature of human experience and keeps alive the openness of human expectation. [...] The variation form is discursive and peripatetic, in flight from all messages and ideologies. Its subject is the adventurer, the picaro, the quick-change artist, the impostor, the phoenix who ever rises from the ashes, the rebel who, defeated, continues his quest, the thinker who doubts perception, who shapes and reshapes reality in search of its inner significance, the omnipotent child who plays with matter as God plays with the universe. Variation [...] shatters appearance into splinters of previously unperceived reality and, by an act of will, reassembles the fragments at the close. The sense of time is effaced — expanded, contracted — by changes in tempo; space and mass dissolve into the barest outline of the harmonic progressions and build up once again into baroque structures laden with richly ornamented patterns. The theme remains throughout as an anchor to prevent fantasy from losing contact with the outer world, but it too dissolves into the memories, images, and feelings which underlie its simple reality.

—Maynard Solomon, *Beethoven*

CONTENTS

*

BOOK THREE: *Is there any such thing as
a complete and finished story?*

We Are Guests of Ancient Time

BOOK ONE:
*A primary attribute of any character
is their relationship to time.*

The boy, remember, is not
myself. In body and mind he
is a dream, a person dreamt
by the land itself, a creature
whose mind is inextricable
from the land's mind, not yet
awakened to consciousness
and separation, not yet. But
look. Any moment now it will
happen.

In nine o'clock darkness a summer moth flits against a streetlamp lens. The shadow it casts is the size of a crow. Prepare to forget this, as you will forget the way you stood several times a season or so outside your own house in the dark and turned to see the windows aglow and the roofline melting off into stars. Prepare to forget your gratitude for the damp of shade. And do not try to explain the restoration of flesh, how the accidental incision grows closed across the thumb's bald face like a smile. Strive to describe only: the clarity of time, the smallness of oceans, the waves that seem to freeze and harden into furrows far below your passing plane, the unknown age of underwater objects laid away in those aqueous attics beyond the undertow. Only minutes ago it was morning. A train was traveling along a river and just offshore a man in a red rowboat stood between his oars to applaud its passing. Don't speak of the carrying, the bearing forward, and the wind the motion makes. Aboard that train a young man, fourteen and black, asleep across two seats, grips a large mechanical camera, the neckstrap coiled at his wrist. Prepare to forget all this and all that we bear home, all that we bring and thought to bring and never thought to bring. I am, as you are, familiar with nonexistence. Only the crow can be said to own all that it sees at the turning in the high desert where the road passes or here in the city amid obstructed streets, and yet from the dogwood trees in the park someone has hung calligraphy. Or left it there, meaning to come back. Try, if you want, to grasp the lives and lifetimes gliding past in windows along the expressway. Why not try? Try, but handle with care the carnival of pilgrims and consumers come from afar to throw a coin, to summon divinity with one clap, two claps, a slow bow, two bows, three. Give thanks for the sulfurous spring, the wrapping of cloth across the breast, the music in the mind and gateway of the ear, green land and black ridges and the swing of the body riding passenger. Give thanks even while you prepare. Prepare to let pass what is sacred in the shrine, the innumerable visits preceding mine and yours. And what is most moving, the movement here of so many before — that too you will let pass. There is no cause to mourn your missing of the rind and the fruit, your loss of the tea leaves and the wheat stalk, the coffee berry and the boats that move in mists upon the water, the paper tassels on a vermilion gate that clatter in the heat like rain. Leave alone the hot wind that quakes along the sidewalk and the young woman who stops, arms flung wide, to face it and laugh. Loosen your grasp and prepare to forget the cold cube of butter in your shirtpocket, carried from a tienda during the hundred-degree siesta. Unclutch the quiet of the city one hour after dawn, let go the watered streets now dry, the day not yet begun, and a boy, strong-limbed, capable, and eager to inhabit his body, to roll and leap and dash and dive until onlookers laugh to see him outrunning every languor. Your son who knows the pleasures of the radio, for whom the imperious deer at Nara do not refuse to bow. Give them your leave, and him, and the green park dotted with droppings. Kettle-like the dusky corridors of the rambling castle quietly hiss in a midday downpour. The boards of the walk again release the resinous odor of dawn. Prepare to forget it all. In shade transpires the soft damp decay as slow as the honey for which you once gave thanks: refined in the papery jaws of bees, distilled in their microscopic saliva, the mouth-warm musk sniffed in its jar. But give thanks again now for the fall of the porcelain honeypot and prepare to forget how you watched your thoughts as if from afar while watching it drop. Forever, almost, it will go on falling, falling, to pop into pieces on the floor. It's done for. Brace yourself and let it go.

Sometime much later the honey explodes.

Variations on the Finding

ERE IS A PICTURE. Here is a child: scrawny boy in Sunday clothes, brown pile of hair that does not fall into the eyes as hair tends to do in descriptions, but juts and bulges asymmetrically.

A bright Sunday morning and the boy stands alone behind a country church in Corralitos, California. Corralitos means "small enclosures." The name originates one October day in 1769 when the men of Spain's Portolá Expedition — scurvy-sick, weary — rest their starving pack mules in this spot while searching for the fabled Port of Monterey.

The boy is five years old. I am the boy.

No. To say I am the boy may be acceptable technically, but impossible. These memories are hardly even mine. I have questions. Can we reclaim — any of us — innocence toward our own first perceptions?

———

THE BOY STARES OVER a low wooden fence into
the apple orchard on the other side: trees upon
trees in the sunlight — trees without end. Within
this moment the boy senses something different.
Something new. Is it because this is the first time
he's ever truly been alone?

The boy decides he'll run away.

Can the act of memory work as a kind of
perforation? Trace a child's outline, press with
fingertips from behind, watch the image come
loose in the hands.

Again, no. The boy is a piece of every situation, every
background. Here: the orange shag carpet of a living
room littered with holiday wrapping and toys, his
fourth Christmas. Here: a highway shoulder's ellipse
of weathered asphalt and a mound of greasy white,
the day he first sees snow, age six. Here: age five and
standing at the edge of sun-bright orchards — the
first time he's ever contemplated running away.
Setting saturates everything.

No one sees him. Not his parents or siblings, not
the many others now praying or singing inside the
church. Let's not lie when we remember. No one

sees the boy, most of all not I: his mute far-off
undreamt of future. I must construct him.

The boy decides he'll run away, as boys and girls do.
He climbs the low wooden fence and his feet sink
deep into apple orchard earth and he sets off
walking while back inside the church Sunday school
begins and nobody notices he's not there. He will be
gone a long time. "Lost," they'll call it.

Where is he going? Where was *I* going? Where did the
boy think he was going?

———

15 October 1769.

MORE THAN SIXTY MEN in the Expedition:
soldiers, muleteers, cartographers, priests, and
Captain Don Gaspar de Portolá himself. They are
in search of Monterey, a natural harbor they've
only read about. They are in sore shape —
starving or sick or both, and several in their
retinue have recently deserted. Overland through
strange rugged country devoid of game, they've
come 450 miles from San Diego. They have
passed through numerous native villages, all
abandoned. Anyway, as men so fixed in their

purpose, the native narratives are unavailable to them. Lately reduced to eating their own mules with a garnish of moldy flour, the Spaniards continue in quest of the elusive Monterey harbor, dragging themselves along. They've traveled inland after camping several days at a place they call Rio del Pajaro near the future township of Watsonville (where I will be born), and now they reach the Corralitos site. Here they behold something previously unknown to Europeans. According to their chief engineer Miguel Costansó, whose diary provides one of the best accounts of the expedition, they find "the largest, highest, and straightest trees that we had seen up to that time. Some of them were four or five yards in diameter. The wood is of a dull, dark, reddish color, very soft, brittle, and full of knots." They are looking at a grove of magnificent coast redwoods.

They call the site La Lagunilla, after a small lagoon nearby. But often on this expedition priest or superior will name a place one thing while soldier calls it something else, and in this case the unofficial name somehow lingers as the Expedition moves on: "Corralitos."

Today some locals surmise that the name derives from those redwood groves, which still grow there. As the Spaniards would have noted, the redwoods stand in circular clusters, forming numerous small enclosures.

So: "Corralitos," where two centuries later a yellow country church stands amid orchards. Where...

One bright Sunday a boy's spiritual life begins.

———

FIVE YEARS OLD, A BOY TRAMPS ALONE through a sea of apple trees, deep in the pleasures of his mind. He has no thought of time. He has no other life. He's become somebody else, in a different place. This is easy because he's so very young.

When we are very young we are largely insane. It is our primary business to be lost in our imaginations. Later on we become lost in time.

We're slow to understand time. To sense and reckon the passing of hours and days — this skill is not inborn. First the world is timeless: all abundance or all scarcity, an ever-recurring present. And much later, finally, we blur into our backgrounds, or they into us. The edges and colors seep and bleed — temporal, spatial, personal — image into image, layer into layer.

So any story may just as well begin with the background of the dead.

P ERHAPS BEGIN THIS STORY with the dead. The
dead are part of the setting, part of the oversaturation
in every old photo. The dead are the background
surface against which a child's shape grows clear. Even
unpeopled scenery contains them: orchard row,
country highway, farmland vista. This includes the
dead of the historical past.

Pen in hand, fingers at keys, my thoughts turn round
and round the dead, round and round a child's first
imaginative flight. Hours, it must have been, although
for me the memory survives as just a few moments,
mirage-like, and maybe of hopelessly personal
significance. Impossibly insular.

There are large things that happen so early on that
later you can only believe you've dreamt them.

I can try, maybe, to extract the boy from dream, but
even if I wished it he won't be separated from what
surrounds him. Corralitos apple trees, yellow country
church, and eight miles west: the vast watery expanse
of Monterey Bay.

And the more definitely I locate boy in setting,
wandering lost and dreaming, the more setting

expands to include the Spaniards wandering lost at Corralitos in 1769, Portolá and his men unable to find the harbor of Monterey, although it lies just eight miles behind them.

First: a brief episode of purely personal significance involving a five-year-old boy in 1983. Second: 18th-century imperial exploration of the so-called New World. These things are unalike until in my imagination the landscape holds them together.

Or rather: Imagination is a landscape unifying unalike things.

Let's wander in this landscape. Isn't that our whole project — to be lost, and yet somehow to see where we stand?

———

1602, nearly two centuries before Portolá.

SPANISH EXPLORER SEBASTIÁN VIZCAÍNO writes an account extolling the virtues of Monterey. A civilian businessman with a taste for mercenary exploits, Vizcaíno has undertaken an epic overseas journey on his own dime, promised the reward of a Manila galleon in the event that he should locate for the crown an ideal Alta California harbor. Vizcaíno christens the great bay in honor of Viceroy Monterey, and describes "a noble harbor, the best port that could be desired...sheltered from all winds" with "many pines for masts and yards, and live oaks and white oaks ... all near the shore."

For this discovery Vizcaíno wins his galleon, and nearly two centuries later the image of his ideal natural harbor still haunts Spain's imperial imagination. Roused to jealousy by Russian explorations along the Pacific coast, the Spanish crown determines to finally claim and secure the spot.

But something is amiss. Vizcaíno's description happens to be so unfaithful to the real geography of the place, so totally different from the bay's actual harborless, windswept vastness, that 167 years later, during their thousand-mile journey overland from San Diego to San Francisco Bay and back, Portolá and his men manage to miss Monterey Bay altogether, despite camping twice on its very shores. From 4 October to 7 October 1769, and again on the night of 27 November, Portolá, Miguel Costansó, and the roughly 62 men of the Expeditionary Corps pass hours and hours staring out at the waters of the bay itself — and they never see it.

From Costansó's diary:

We did not know what to think of the situation. A

port so famous as that of Monterey, so celebrated
and so talked of in its time by energetic skillful
and intelligent men, expert sailors who came
expressly to reconnoiter these coasts by order of the
monarch — is it possible to say that it has not been
found after the most careful and earnest efforts,
carried out at the cost of much toil and fatigue? Or
is it admissible to think that it has been filled up or
destroyed in the course of time?

   The accounts of General Sebastián Vizcaíno
and his contemporary historians give the port of
Monterey as being 37° north latitude ...

   Having examined the whole coast step by step,
we have not the least fear that it may have escaped
our diligence and search.

Being precisely where they meant to be, they believed
themselves lost.

———

"ONE IS TAUGHT," writes John Berger, "to
oppose the real to the imaginary, as though the
first were always at hand and the second distant, far
away. This opposition is false. Events are always at
hand. But the coherence of these events — which is
what one means by reality — is an imaginative
construction."

Description is everything, and it is more innate than we usually realize. All that we see we try to describe to ourselves.

And maybe, when we are still young, we look for ourselves in every story. While later on, being lost in time, we have the advantage of surrendering to the inviolable landscapes and lost time of other narratives.

———

P ERHAPS, WHILE WALKING in an apple orchard, a small boy begins to levitate.

The coherence of events — which is what one means by reality — is an imaginative construction.

The boy is levitating. The boy realizes he did not climb that fence now far, far behind him, but levitated over it. And now, his feet pedaling aimlessly beneath him, the boy goes upward through the interlocking canopies of apple trees, through branches bulbous with fruit. Upward into soft air and sunlight, orchards ruled out neatly below, his shadow rippling tree to tree.

And soon, looking down, he can see all geography, all history, all time. Old California: its first peoples grinding acorns, weaving baskets, harvesting grasshoppers, renewing the soil with fires. And then the late-comers, the namegivers. He sees Portolá's bedraggled men, their sickly mules.

No one has told them that the crown revoked Sebastián Vizcaíno's prize galleon. That they hung his mapmaker for forgery. Even when faced with the actual bay, even starving, even diseased, the Expedition cannot face its own motivating error — cannot face that Vizcaíno's words, upon which the Expedition relies, are fiction.

————

CALIFORNIA, EPICENTER OF DREAM and error, was born in fiction.

1510 Madrid, two and a half centuries before Portolá: Garci Rodríguez de Montalvo publishes *La Sergas de Esplandián*, or *The Exploits of Esplandián*. It's a knocked-off sequel to the chivalrous Portuguese romance *Amadís of Gaul*, which Montalvo has translated to huge popularity. So enduring are *Amadís* and *Esplandián*, that a century later Miguel de Cervantes will blame both books for withering Don Quixote's brain.

In *Esplandián,* the titular hero and his father Amadís, while defending Constantinople against a pagan siege, find themselves attacked by one Calafía, fearsome Queen of California. This lady's kingdom is itself a fearsome place, "an island," as Montalvo describes it, "on the right hand of the Indies [and] very near to the terrestrial paradise." California is thick with horrible griffins all lusting for battle, who are known to pluck men from the ground, carry them up to the strato- sphere, and then send them falling. Amid the griffins live heartless Amazons who wield weapons made of the island's only metal (yes, California gold). These women warriors trap young griffins and raise them for warfare in their caves, feeding them "with the men whom they took prisoners, and with the boys to whom they gave birth."

———

F ROM HIS EARLY-16TH-CENTURY LETTERS to the Spanish royalty, written during the explorations that led him to Baja California, it is clear that Hernán Cortés expected to find an island of Amazons in the region.

"It may have been in derision," says one California history, "that Spanish explorers gave to a barren and hostile place the name of the fabled land of gold they had hoped to find."

9 December 1769.

W ITH ONLY 14 SACKS OF FLOUR remaining to
the expeditionary team, many of the men having
taken ill with scurvy, two native Indian guides
having deserted, and two muleteers having gone
missing 13 days prior, the Portolá Expedition, after
wandering north and south, plants in the sand of the
beach at Carmel a large cross fashioned of driftwood,
engraved with the words: *Escarba: al pié hallarás un
escrito*, or "Dig! At the foot thou wilt find a writing."
Beneath the cross is buried a letter written by Miguel
Costansó:

> *The land-expedition that set out from San Diego*
> *on 14 July 1769 under the command of the*
> *Governor of California, Don Gaspar de Portolá*
> *reached the foot of the Sierra de Santa Lucía on*
> *13 September ... It completed the passage of*
> *the mountain range, going completely round it, on*
> *1 October and on the same day came in sight of the*
> *Punta de Pinos. On the 7th of the same month*
> *having already examined the Punta de Pinos and*
> *the bays to the north and south of it*
> *without finding any indications of the port of*
> *Monterey it decided to go forward in search of the*

port. On 30 October the expedition came in sight
of...the port of San Francisco. The expedition ...
[turned back] believing that the port of Monterey
might possibly be found within the Sierra de
Santa Lucía and fearing that the port might have
been passed without having been seen. The
expedition arrived again at this Punta on the
27th of the same month. From that day to
the present 9 December the expedition was
engaged in searching within the mountains for the
port of Monterey. ... Finally now disappointed
and despairing of finding the port after so many
endeavors labors and hardships and without other
provisions than fourteen sacks of flour the
expedition sets out today from this bay for San
Diego. Pray thou Almighty God to guide it.

They leave the cross standing there on the beach at
Carmel. The Expedition is a failure, though by
accident they have found and christened the bay of
San Francisco.

———

* Punta de Pinos is in fact the southern-most point of Monterey
Bay.

HOPING TO PURGE DON QUIXOTE'S library of the books that have caused his madness, Cervantes's barber and priest come upon the first blameworthy title: "This," says the barber, "is *The Exploits of Esplandián.*" And the priest answers, "Open that window and throw it into the yard. The first faggot on the bonfire we're going to make."

Earlier, Cervantes pictures the readerly exertions that have ruined Don Quixote's brain, his overexposure to chivalrous verbiage like: "The lofty heavens which with their stars divinely fortify you in your divinity, and make you meritorious of the merits merited by your greatness." Don Quixote's madness and the vain labors, hardships, disappointment, and despair of the Portolá Expedition desperately dependent upon Vizcaíno's descriptions — these share a culprit: bad style.

———

THE BOY LEVITATES UPWARD STILL, slung securely in a hammock of air, some invisible force bearing him higher.

Years later, when the boy is a young man, he will sit in prolonged self-confinement putting down words, reading, putting down further words. This too will be a form of levitation. All that time he will ask himself: *What do I mean to say? How will I manage to say it? How, in the saying, will I banish untruth from the expression?* This is the same as asking: *What is a voice? What is a style?*

And he will learn, slowly, that what characterizes bad style is not the length of one's sentences, or the use of adjectives or adverbs, or brazenly resorting to arcane vocabulary. He will learn that what characterizes bad style is mendacity. That bad stylists are careless with the truth at the heart of their subject. He will learn that a calculating mercenary lives in us all, and bad style is the failure to root him out. You can't write with something else on your mind. Having something else on their minds, bad stylists miss their own point altogether.

Bad style is the failure to get lost, the failure to loosen the grip on one's own design and wander abroad in the sudden country of the material at hand. It is a failure to surrender to the moment and place in which you stand, to the disciplinary truth that nothing can guarantee success, and so it's an incapacity to surprise oneself. Bad style is claiming you've made a journey which your own lines reveal you never made. In the end, bad style is always a form of lying. And lying differs in substance and quality (if not in aspect) from imaginative creation.

[Style is] sensibility and technique distinctively brought together. Jeanette Winterson *(Art Objects).*

In the pursuit of clarity, style reveals itself. ... [Style is] an expression of the interest you take in the making of every sentence. Verlyn Klinkenborg *(Several Short Sentences on Writing).*

[Style is] a language as precise as possible, both in choice of words and in expression of the subtleties of thought and imagination. Italo Calvino *(Six Memos for the Next Millennium).*

[Style is] the supposition that, despite everything, a melody can be looked for and sometimes found. [...] It requires and encourages a talent for endurance and an ease with time. Style is very close to music. [...] Style comes from within, yet style has to borrow its assurance from another time and then lend it to the present, and the borrower has to leave a pledge with that other time. The passionate present is invariably too short for style. John Berger *(Here Is Where We Meet).*

The beginner should approach style warily, realizing that it is oneself one is approaching, no other. Strunk and White *(The Elements of Style).*

———

F INALLY, BACK AT THE CHURCH the boy's parents and fellow congregants raise the alarm. The church bells clang, quaking over the orchards. The boy hears, utterly strange, the sound of a name being called. Unfamiliar voices. Down there, very far below, a strange woman and her child stand in the orchard, waving. How do they see him up here? How do they know him?

He moves toward them, confused, wind whistling across his forehead, visible streamers of sunlight flowing upward through his outspread limbs, leaves of apple trees crashing in his ears, cluttering his sight with green. Then he's standing at the woman's side and she is bending down very close. *Your parents are awfully worried about you.*

She takes his hand.

———

B ACK ON THE GROUND, THE BOY is a pinpoint on a map, a microscopic divot on a quadrangular mass of pink labeled NORTH AMERICA. From the solar perspective, beholding the watery globe itself, the boy is not even a divot, not even a dot, not so much as a speck. And yet, from whatever unthinkable distance, in the context of whatever infinite scale, out of whatever epoch long since foretold, doesn't the boy shed, in some way, an uncanny residue somewhat like light? Mustn't he? Don't we all?

The boy, remember, is not me. A mass of incident and impression, he is someone else's story, not yet autobiographical. He has no narrative.

Body and mind the boy has been, until this moment, a dream, a person dreamt by the land itself, a creature not yet awakened to consciousness. But this is the day it happens. Look. There he goes. The land itself has seen him and — all at once: a change.

The boy is no longer just a dream the land is having. There comes a waking and now boy and place are distinct — still interwoven, still blurred forever at the edges, but no longer indivisible.

How long was the boy gone? How far did the boy go? Called down, called forward out of his own native timelessness, he has learned, somehow, that despite all efforts and assertions, despite all our many small enclosures, it is imaginative structures that carry the day, that dreaming and being lost undergird our every moment.

Dig! You will find a writing.

Years later still, the young man is a father. "If I stayed up all day and all night," his five-year old son announces, "I could watch my body grow!"

The father buys a large colorful book for his son. The back page folds out and there is a clock with moveable hands. He moves the boy's hands on the hands of the clock.

We are good heirs and good benefactors.

———

ON THE BEACH AT CARMEL, having found the Spaniards' cross, the native people, the Ohlone, bedecked it with necklaces of mussel shells. They encircled it with arrows stuck point-first into the sand. It became a shrine.

The Caretaker's Variations

NOVEMBER.   The other night I dreamt of bucks — massive racks on their heads, noses wet and dark like squashed prunes. One of them had great curvilinear antlers, branching outward to an eight-foot diameter, nearly touching again at the tips. His nostrils smoked. He set his jaw and stared at me: eyes black, hollow. Then he turned and I saw his flanks, his reverse-jointed legs stepping, his painted tail. He lowered his head in his grazing walk, but still I saw the antlers: yellow gyrosphere floating into orchard darkness.

I've been seeing the genuine article each morning as I leave before dawn to deliver newspapers — young, magisterial buck ambling through the walnut grove across the main road. He's been in the same place at the same hour for three days in a row — once alone (when I saw him leap a wire fence in one supple motion, like liquid thrown in an arc), once accompanied by a single stag, and once attended by two big does and a handful of fawns. My headlights do not startle him. He floats calmly away from the light, unalarmed, head low, fellow mammal. His antlers stand straight from his skull in a narrow, curving V four feet tall. He is an eminence, a spirit, a rhythm embodied, the land given shape and gesture and muscle, a grace, a bodhisattva, a talisman — and to me: an illumination on the page of my life, illustrious ancientness, an old-world character in living ink, signifying all is well. I've looked it up in my symbols book: the stag, known for its fleetness and sharp senses, which make capture difficult, is an attribute of hearing. Ah, to learn to hear. To learn to listen.

In the dark mornings, walking out to the car when all is blackness and even the stars seem asleep, I hear them stepping through the oak leaves — three or four of them at least — slipping back away from my strange form, sometimes hopping toward the north pasture where they collect in a stronghold of community. Hopping. The measured beat and crunch of their feet, trailing off. And, if I truly listen: the taut snap and whisper of muscle and limb.

———

ON SATURDAY WE WALKED SOUTH along the property's edge, through the grove where I'd seen the buck, and into Briones, the vast and brambly open space across the road. Just beside the gate at the front of the property, in a tangle of star thistle and bunch grass: the fresh skeleton of a fawn, feathery with shredded fur and headless. I bent close and saw the vertebrae — gentle animal architecture. Saw the tiny ungulate feet still intact. The parcel of the belly ripped open and tongued clean of tendon and gut. Wondered where the skull had gone — the coveted morsel, carried off in coyote jaws for the more assiduous feeding. Little ravaged animal, backbone ending in a gnarled fist. Tiny feet, limp and crisscrossed in the dirt.

We walked for an hour or so, climbing to a view of Mount Diablo eight miles east. The day was clear and bright, smelling of sun-warmed dirt, pine, eucalyptus.

———

THE FIRST TRUE STORM OF THE SEASON has passed us now. A good muscular storm: two days of wind and rain, muggy gusts that broke limbs from the oaks and brought down power lines.

Night before last, in the wind and torrent, insects thronged our front door: beetles wild in exodus from the sopping leaves, spiders groggy and sprawling in the cracks of our sill, and a slow sleepwalking salamander the color of coffee — green bulbous eyes, limbs that paddle the air softly as though swimming. (Do the amphibious creatures live the elements in converse order: crawling through water, swimming through air?) It stretched its curving length across my palm before I set it down in the dirt clearing. Later you reminded me that they respire through their skin and shouldn't be touched because the salt of our human bodies harms them.

———

THIS MORNING, SIX O'CLOCK, driving back to the property in the moments just before dawn: a luminous, low-spreading fog over the narrow Reliez Valley at the mouth of Briones. Blue smoke rolling over dark fields. Somewhere within it: a light. As if dawn begins in the earth itself, glow of steam unfurling from the soil.

———

EVENING. DEEP, DARK AUTUMN EVENING in which the night ages at a rate startling to us creeping humans. Cold air. Not a light in these valley hills. The crunch of an animal in the blackness: crumpled oak leaf under hoof, paw, talon, claw. Inside, I am snug and lamplit, bent at the kitchen table next to a taper candle's glow. The kettle sings, aluminum rattling, the water in it still boiling as I pour. Two steaming cups. Then two steps down into the bedroom and through the door to the study where you are at work with papers and books. A "thank you" and a "sweetheart" from you, and your lips at my wrist, mine to your head: the crown of dark curls lavender-scented, and in concord with the unnamable smell of you.

Another evening inside with a journal and some books, earth-colored tea, herbal infusion over the tongue and between the cheeks, steam of the tipped cup touching our faces. We'll fall back into autumn thoughts, leafy mound of the mind, mulch of the heart and soul. Sod of body accepting the falling detritus from the tree of thought, the tree of feeling.

Now I am in it. Now I am leaf that falls in the dark of night. Now I am tree: many-limbed body in the blackness, past which the big-pupiled animals slip, crunching. Then they stop, one paw dangling, one hoof. Head up and black eyes slurping at shadows, listening to the sound of someone else in the darkness, sharer of the night, being who listens to them.

To hear the oceanic blood in my ears, the health of this body vibrant against silence. To lean into the space above this kitchen table, enclosed by it, at home in it for perhaps the first time. To step inside through a door, and inside again, and find the rooms filling up with stars, the walls stretching as high and wide as an autumnal sky, the breath of these lungs pluming into animal shapes — all that is inward flowing outward ... Deer and hawk, lamb's ear, laurel, footbridge, flagstone, mud field, horse print, asparagus weed, farm road, goat laughter, hinge moan, roof skitter, barn cat, crooked ladder, bale and flake, grain bucket full of rainwater, streak of galaxy, greening storm, the kitten's dish and a soft thumbless paw kittening the palm of the hand. Contact.

I feel better than I have felt in weeks. Limpid. Lucid. Luminous. And everything seems to speak my thanks. I feel more alive than I have felt in seasons. And this night is like an animal's glowworm eyes.

———

Last WEEK ON THE HILLSIDE, bending to scoop up a pile of leaf, I caught the soft glister of a steely thing — something twisted, coiled like a length of narrow spring. Looking closer I saw the taper at both ends, and prodding it with the rake till it turned I made out the copper-colored back. A little snake bunched into a stiff figure-eight. Dead, I thought. He was no thicker than a pencil, no longer than a normal rubber-band cut once. His belly was the thing I'd seen first: tiny horizontal bands from nose to tail, bright silver and black, and with a sheen like polished wire. On his back: two or three vertical stripes running his whole length, a lighter orange against the reptilian copper.

I took a piece of twig and lifted him from the leaves and brought him closer to find the tiny tongue lapping blindly at the air. The flavor of my presence. Then saw the rigid body slinking over the twig, every infinitesimal scale separating till the body grew in a dripping way. I carried him up the hill and laid him down in a bare place and watched him stretch sleepily to his full length — three times what I'd judged it to be. In a moment or two he moved back toward his winter blanket of leaf, buried his head like a groggy child prematurely awakened. Like I was the goading parent he didn't yet wish to see. Back to his hillside snake dreams, his soil-warmth, his four-month torpor of empty-belly silence and sunless contentment.

———

FEBRUARY.   Last Saturday we walked across the road and up the path to the little hillside edge of Briones. We cut along a footpath up the face of the slope, stepping in dried horse prints. The clarifying wind tumbled from the crest and over us. You were close in front of me, taking long climbing strides. I tried to place my steps in the spots your feet lifted from, and was reminded of the smallness of your body. We stood at the crest looking westward along the long Alhambra Valley. The folds of green hills — two rows of them mirroring each other.

"I love that view," you said.

I said I loved it too.

At the little rise behind us, you discovered a thin path. No more than a deer path, snaking up into a thicket of bay laurels. I followed you along it into the trees, where the path vanished beneath crunching leaves six inches deep. We stepped about under the trees, over broken limbs and tangled shrubs. The space was like a room, walled on all sides by narrow trunks and hanging leaves.

"This is where the deer come to sleep," I said,

crunching in circles, looking for antlers.

We moved around in that space, turning, feeling it.
The canopy whispered. Then, together, at the same
moment, we both caught sight of a white thing among
the fallen leaves. It sat nosing a downed limb. An oblong
skull, the size and shape of a small football. We
crouched on two sides of it. We looked without touching
it.

"A deer," I said.

"Is it?"

I grasped it lightly between middle finger and thumb,
touching it in the place the ears had been, and turned it
over. It was as light as an empty cup. We both made
little sounds of awe as we looked at the teeth: large flat
things, like double molars. They lined the mouth in a
perfect U and were beginning to rot. The lower hinge of
jaw was missing.

"A deer," I said.

"With teeth like that? I didn't think they'd have teeth
so big. Where were the antlers?"

"Maybe here," I said.

But the skull looked too small for antlers. And I
thought perhaps this was the head from the tiny
skeleton down at the property's edge. The size looked
right. So did the state of decay — it had been several
months. I pictured the silent coyote trotting across the
road in the deep of night, his jaw agape around this little
head, climbing the hill to this spot beneath the trees,

lying down with the skull between his paws and lapping at the delicate fat.

I turned the skull upright, pointed to the hole at its back, inlet to the hollow brain box. "Here's where the backbone connected. Look how clean it is in there," I said. Saw the predator tonguing it white. Saw rat and coon and possum coming for days afterward to finish the work.

I laid the skull in place again, fit it back into its pocket of leaf. There were faint gray zigzags like stitch-marks in the bone of the crown.

We left the skull and stepped out of the trees. But I see it up there now, darkened by today's rain, its perfect teeth set against the leaves as though eating them. I picture the slow rot week after week — leaves piling up, white bone sinking until it disappears, taken in by the soil and by the earth.

Outsideness, or: My Phone Says "Searching…" *

1.

O NE EVENING at a family gathering, I found myself alone in the living room, my four-year-old son asleep on my chest, while the rest of the family socialized in the nearby kitchen. On an end-table, a book caught my eye. It was well out of arm's reach. I didn't want to wake my son, but I didn't want to fall asleep myself, and that book looked interesting. Finally, after a quandary of several minutes, a solution occurred to me. I fished the cell phone from my pocket and dialed a number on my "contacts" list. Beyond the living room wall, in the kitchen, I heard another phone begin to bleat. Then my sister-in-law's voice: "I have a call from Mark Cunningham," she announced to the people in the kitchen. "Isn't he in the living room?"

She answered. We were both holding our phones to our ears, but we could hear one another through the wall. Quietly, I asked my sister-in-law to ask my wife to come into the living room.

A second later, my wife appeared. At the sight of our sleeping darling she gave a lovely, mothering smile.

---

* Based on remarks delivered for the Oregon Legacy Author Series in Lincoln City, Oregon. Speakers are asked, "How does the Oregon landscape influence your work?"

Then she handed me the book. Our boy could go on sleeping, while I read contentedly.

The wonders of technology.

———

M Y SHORT-DISTANCE CALL WAS a privately satirical gesture. My anecdote about it here is meant to be equally satirical. It's absurd, of course, to phone a relative who's sitting in an adjacent room. I'm reminded of some words from our late great Librarian of Congress Daniel Boorstin. "Technology," Boorstin said, "insulates and isolates. While [it] seems to bring us together, it does so only by making new ways of separating us from one another. ... The future will be a world of millions of private compartments."* Boorstin was writing in 1978, but we of the present, living as we are in the age of the office cubicle, the home PC, the blue-tooth-enabled commuter car, and the Instagram profile, know very well what he means about "compartments."

Our technologies have always promised in some way or other to regenerate us. This is precisely their allure. With a faster car, we will travel farther, have greater freedom and more adventures; with a good e-reading device, we will read more; with a better smartphone we

———

* From Boorstin's "The Republic of Technology and the Limits of Prophecy"

will extend our social and professional reach — and be reached more often.

In my novel, *Perpetua's Kin*, the main character Benjamin Lorn, growing up in a tiny Iowa town in the late 1800s, finds this promise of technological regeneration in the Internet of his day: the telegraph.

> At the copper-edged counter in Perpetua's Wabash depot Benjamin had stood with his father, sometimes his mother, and watched Mr. Mueller, depot man, postal clerk, and operator, tapping signals into the wire by use of a trim lever key. The key made glottic clicking sounds and Mr. Mueller's green visor glistered as he canted his head to listen. His tapping formed no clear pattern but a body could speak to anyone in the country — even as far as California — by that method. Or so Benjamin had learned. It seemed pure conjuration. It offered wonder even grownups could not foreswear. The boy could think of no other thing with such a claim, whose magic would not die no matter how aged or wise a person got.
>
> The humming wires followed King Street along Perpetua's town square and continued west to the track by the depot. From there they trued themselves to the railroad. Standing in his father's store or at the depot platform Benjamin watched them bellying pole

to pole and onward to distances unreckoned. Twice, three times a day the trains thundered through that way, to vanish at the narrow place on the horizon. It always left the wires swaying overhead, droning sorcery. "Wind makes em hum," his father told him, but Benjamin would not believe this. At heart he knew the sound to be voice of a secret energy. Already he felt eternity in the wires.

And so Benjamin resolves to become an operator, to live a railroading life of adventurous travel from station to station, a "boomer's" existence — *Westward Ho!* — working the wires as he goes, outpacing the forces of time, geography, and his dark family history by essentially uploading himself into a wire.

> Always going, purely present, blind to all preceding. ... He wants to be the humming wire, outside time. To let nothing cling to him.

Late in his travels, arriving in Pendleton, Oregon, Benjamin meets — and enters the employ of — a lesser tycoon of the railroad and telegraph, a mad prophet of the new (I wholly invented this character, incidentally). "The railroad and telegraph shatter," the man tells Benjamin,

> wholly shatter our tidy conceptions of time. To wit, the locomotive has carried us in a few

short decades from life by crop to life by clock.
Can we yet comprehend the implications of
such a shift? The immense consequences in
our history, the very consciousness of our
race? Think of it, my friend, for the man awake
in India this very moment is a different day. It
is tomorrow. Yet we may touch him by wire in
a matter of moments. We may reach from this
day to that futurity. What have we done then
but overthrow time? — and geography, time's
confederate. Even mountains needn't
encumber us.

The same man tells Benjamin: "We have learned
irreverence toward sun and season." And this last
statement is borrowed — repurposed — from Neil
Postman's book *Amusing Ourselves to Death*, a landmark
and, yes, amusing work of cultural commentary,
published in the 1980s, about television's effect on
American culture. What beautiful and disturbing words
Postman's are. They've haunted me, those words, since I
first read them years ago. How could I resist smuggling
them into my own work? — putting them into the
mouth of a frontier technologist, a character meant to
suggest the first inklings, here in the West, of the
consciousness that would give us Silicon Valley. It's as a
Westerner, as a native of this edge of the continent, that
Postman's words really get to me. We have learned
irreverence toward sun and season.

2.

SOME FRIENDS OF MINE, parents of a five-year-old girl, once told me of their daughter's confusion while driving around Pennsylvania during a family visit there. Her parents had pointed out some Pennsylvania mountains. "Where are they?" the girl kept saying. "I can't see them. I *can't see* them!" She was looking right at them. But this was a girl who had grown up in view of Mount Hood, Mount Saint Helens, Mount Adams, and Mount Rainier (11,250 feet, 8,400 feet, 12,300 feet, and 14,400 feet respectively).

The native Westerner (the one who stays anyway) enjoys a special inheritance. We tend to understand a thing or two, down in our bones, about mountains and canyons, landscapes and long views, the vastness of the natural realms. "I have never been able to refrain," wrote Wallace Stegner, one of our greatest writers, "from telling easterners that Mount Washington, their pride, could be set down in the Grand Canyon — in a *ditch* — and never show above the rim. ... Whatever he may *not* know, a Westerner is bound to know geography."

I'd put it a little more starkly: the Westerner is well acquainted with the naked, grand, unnerving face of the earth — and what that suggests about our place in the order of things. Beyond any actual wilderness experiences (which I'd guess most of us have had in lucky abundance), we're well acquainted with the experience of driving for five, six, ten hours and seeing out our window far more landscape (often stunningly scenic) than buildings. I remember being rightly horrified, in a deep existential way — being reduced nicely to size, you might say — the first time I crossed the agoraphobic deserts of Nevada. On Washington's Highway 14, as you head east from the Columbia River Gorge into the forbidding glacial scablands on your way to Walla Walla, you pass a sign I particularly like: "Next gas 87 miles." Stylistically, existentially, that's a remarkable message: a little forlorn, but straight-up, no apologies.

"Destinies, outlined against the basic earth. That is the story we all write in the American West, whether in memory or on the white canyons of paper." That's Ivan Doig, another great writer from this side of the Missouri.

We live, out here, in almost daily consciousness of what you might call the *irrevocable reality of human remoteness.* The wilderness, should it find you inadequately prepared, can eat you up — quite literally if you happen to be, say, in Grizzly country. After a point, it will not matter that you started out in a road-ready SUV with a full tank, a GPS, and a smartphone.

———

T HE WRITER SVEN BIRKERTS, in his magnificent 1994 book, *The Gutenberg Elegies*, prophesied of our technological future:

> It will be harder and harder ... to step free of our mediating devices. There will be people who will never in their lives have the experience that was, until our time, the norm — who will never stand in isolated silence among trees and stones, out of shouting distance of any other person, with no communication implement, forced to confront the slow, grainy momentum of time passing.

Most of *The Gutenberg Elegies*, read today, shows Birkerts to be an uncannily accurate prophet. Our daily lives, over-connected and short on focus, bear out many of his predictions from nearly thirty years ago. But in this particular passage he writes like an easterner (which, as a citizen of Boston, he is). What I mean to say is Birkerts has forgotten, as urban easterners tend to do, that he lives in just one tiny, non-representative patch of the continent. People who will never in their lives stand in isolated silence among trees and stones? Certainly there are already such people in the U.S. — hordes of them, probably, in the urban northeast. But the daily consciousness of the person living in *this* part of the country, here in the West (more specifically perhaps, it comes of being *born* here), often endows that person with a certain exceptionalism when it comes to the technological totality that Birkerts forecasts. Our expansive, still largely "unbuilt" Western landscapes are unlikely to be wholly subjugated to our communication technologies any time soon. And the Western consciousness is one awake, for the most part, to a natural majesty and magnificence that abides, in glorious indifference, amid and around our screen-addled, electronic, technologized lives.

Even from the swarming city of Portland, where I live, I can be in that wild, isolated silence whose absence Birkerts mourns — in less than an hour. It's a short walk along a mostly deserted forest path before my cell phone ceases to do me any good. Only a little farther on, and I'm well out of shouting range, unlikely to see another person for hours, if not days.

———

Stegner again:

> In an open country everyone is a traveler;
> most Westerners develop that habit of
> covering ground in gargantuan chunks. I
> suspect that the man who contemplates empty
> landscape while he drives his own car has
> something of a spiritual advantage on the one
> who, boxed in a subway or bus, contemplates

tomorrow's news in the five o'clock final of
some tabloid. I have no statistics on ulcers, but
I have convictions and some evidence.

3.

ERE'S ANOTHER SLICE OF *Perpetua's Kin,* in
which a sickly Benjamin Lorn travels by train
through the Western barrens, on his way
back to Iowa:

Eastward by rail across country fit to pry the
soul agape, along brindled deserts and on
against long horizon seas of sage star thistle
soapbrush fireweed — volcanic cinder piled up
in cones to block the sun. Elsewhere along
morainal slopes the queer red pumice reposes
in fingerlike crags, a sort of petrified desert
Christmas tree — mantled, these scenes, with
dusting of snow.

A body goes with senses armed. A body
misses nothing for everything leaps. Finding
you sick or tired the country insists no less. In
shuddering seat, in heat and torpor, Benjamin
tries to dim his eyes. No use. He is a flexing
eyeball. Ringing eardrum. The country stands
in a shout. All emptiness and yet no oblivion.
It throws you back on yourself.

That could be a description — and maybe it is, after all — of my own response to the geography of my native West. *A body goes with senses armed. The landscape throws you back on yourself.*

The writer Wendell Berry has said: "There is an intimacy the mind makes with the place it awakens in." As I feel it, the West, which for me meant Northern California until my late twenties, and now means our grand Northwest, is a world to prime the imagination. One becomes a flexing eyeball, a ringing eardrum. My ideas, as a writer, never flow with quite the same fluidity and magical appeal as they do while on a long, long drive through the open country of Oregon.

———

Mᴀ MAIN POINT HERE HAS, I think, something to do with the question of proximity. The proximity, for each of us, of the vast, magisterial, and often forbidding wilds and open spaces of the West — this proximity unites us in a special kind of understanding, and with that comes an instilled skepticism concerning the faux-proximity our technologies promise. (While mindful of the various types of Gold Rush the West has forever been heir to, I've always found it interesting and ironic that the Internet revolution — an entirely *indoor* revolution, irreverent to sun and season — should have originated here.)

As Westerners we are, despite our devices, inhabitants of a world so much larger than ourselves; the evidence is in those long views, punctuated with towering mountain peaks, that we find on our very doorsteps. And I submit that we are acquainted with things — remoteness, aloneness, vast superhuman forces and presences, the silence of trees and stones, the ancient mysteries of the wild — that are the quintessential opposites of what we have come to understand in our technologized, hyper-connected age, as "progress," or as pragmatic, profitable human "evolution." What does a forest path have to do with one's tally of Instagram followers or hits per day?

If we are not, at heart, different out here, then at least our geography, being as different — as *distinctive* — as it is, would have us be so. The land itself implores us to stand apart, if only in a spiritual way, if only in the sense of seeing a larger picture. Call it *Outsideness*, this special consciousness. The terrains of the West manifest a geological scale that utterly decimates human chronology, and so also, to an extent, the significance of human industry, etc.

"What are we in such wastes?" asks the mad tycoon in my novel. "Where can we be bound? We creep small and wayward like flies on a billiard table." His own answer is to proselytize: the telegraph will save us from ourselves and our geographical condition! The telegraph will "ease the ravages of time!" Through that magical wire, "we may unstick ourselves and crawl no more!" It's a message very much alive in the evangelizing of today's technologists, those partisans of the compartmentalized life Daniel Boorstin described back in 1978. Salvation via fiber optic cables!

Well, *we* know better. In the shadow of our snow-capped volcanoes here, on our rugged Western cliff-edge above the sea, we look not as much to the ambitious Europe that so molded the culture of our eastern seaboard, as to the inward-directed ancient East, and like good Buddhists we know that we are small. Yes, and then in spite of (or perhaps because of) this humbling, this clearing of vision, we feel, also, that this West — more spacious than a dream — is a world to unlock our potentialities.

And what potentialities are those?

———

AMID THE HUBBUB OF JANGLING cellphones, of 500 million online tweets per day, of revved-up search engines and frantic status updates, we Westerners, we Oregonians, are only too well acquainted with no-coverage zones. While we stand before a thundering waterfall, or tread the icy waters of a mountain stream in the heat of summer, or watch the spray on the haystack rocks offshore, our phones say simply "Searching ... searching."

And we smile. For once, our gadgets have got it truly right. Our geography reminds us of the greater search to be had — greater values, greater visions, more clear-sighted, more substantial ways to spend the short time we're given.

Guests & Passengers: Variations on Time in Literature, *or: What Does an Imaginative Writer Really Do, Really?*

1.

Narrative and Time

I T IS THE MORNING OF SEPTEMBER 11TH. In Massachusetts, a thirty-three-year-old man — a man regarded with some suspicion by his neighbors — sits down in his bedroom in his parents' attic and writes the following words:

> Autumnal mornings, when the feet of
> countless sparrows are heard like rain-drops
> on the roof by the boy who sleeps in the
> garret.

This is Henry David Thoreau, writing in his journal.

———

I T IS THE MORNING OF SEPTEMBER 11TH. From a dingy fifth-floor room in the Latin Quarter of Paris an impoverished young foreigner and native German-speaker, a man raised as a girl and christened after the

Virgin Mother, painstakingly writes a letter, in his elementary French, to a famous sculptor:

> It is not only to do a study that I have come to you, — it was in order to ask you: how must one live? And you have replied: by working. And this I understand well. I see that to work is to live without dying.

This is Rainer Maria Rilke, writing to Auguste Rodin.

———

I T IS SEPTEMBER 11TH. In a room somewhere in central Europe, a man known for his surly temper and slovenly habits scrawls the following words across a sheet of letter paper:

> Heaven rules over the destiny of men and monsters (literally, human and inhuman beings), and so it will guide me, too, to the better things of life.

This is Ludwig van Beethoven, writing to Elsie von der Recke.

———

I say, "It is September 11th" and turn to you. How do you continue the tale?

The discrete September 11ths just described — each discreetly punctuating the span of nearly a century — resist placement within the continuum where, willingly or not, we all have come to live since the latter-day earth-shaking events of one single morning. Falling between 1811 and 1902, each of the above September 11ths remains isolated by era and substance and we can't quite make them align with our cosmology for that particular date. Each refuses to fit, for us, under the supertitle of "September 11th."

Here, in a way that affects us all, we see the inextricable nature of narrative and time. In this case, for most of us there is one primary "September 11th" overriding every other. The date and its attached narrative together have become a kind of still-frame, shaping our sense of what a single day means and will mean from now on. This narrative appears to freeze time. And we wonder, can the calendric designation "September 11th" ever again stand alone, apart from — and without reference to — the powerful global narrative that the events of one single day imprinted upon it?

How, over time, might time itself affect the narrative?

———

WHAT IS NARRATIVE BUT A WAY, first of all, of factoring time? The earliest English novel bears on its title page the promise of such a factoring: "The Life and Strange Surprising Adventures of Robinson Crusoe, of York, Mariner: Who lived Eight and Twenty Years, all alone in an un-inhabited Island on the Coast of America…" Years — twenty-eight or otherwise — are often the concern. And with narrative we rescue our experience from the randomizing effects of those years, mitigating trauma's impact through the clarity of narrative retrospection. "It's years beyond the worst of it," begins Mitchell S. Jackson's memoiristic novel *The Residue Years*, about a mother in the grip of drug addiction and her son's misspent youth as a dealer, "and it's your time, Mom, a time of head starts and new starts and starting and going and not stopping — of re-dos and fixes, of gazing at full moons and quarter-moons and seeing what before were phantasms for-reals."

It is through narrative that we pick up scattered pieces and neatly distribute them across time according to a broader, more privileged chronological view than the one we're permitted while in the thick of emotion and event. It is through narrative that we find cause connected to effect. "Later you look back and see one thing foretold by another," writes Jayne Anne Phillips. "But when you're young, those connections are secrets; everything you know is secret from yourself." That's from Phillips's multi-generational *Machine Dreams*, a novel of devastating authenticity, about hard lessons learned and relearned across the familial dysfunction of an American century serially consumed in war.

It is narrative that gives shape to the days, the years, and it is narrative we invoke to justify our making of decisions, our taking of actions intended, ostensibly, to steer us through time's perils. "Instead of drifting along toward tragedy, we will set a course toward safety," said President George W. Bush on March 17, 2003, announcing the ultimatum that preceded the U.S. invasion of Iraq.

It is through narrative that we strive to track time's influences upon us and upon those people and things we love. *Where did we come from?* is the first question underlying the symbolic storytelling logic of so many myths. *Where do we go from here?* Mythic questions are almost always questions about time, just as the Book of Genesis, from its first words, records the ancient impulse to trace time to its roots: "In the beginning..."

It is through narrative that memory finds the voice to assert itself against time:

> I remember my childhood names for grasses
> and secret flowers. I remember where a toad
> may live and what time the birds awaken in
> the summer — and what trees and seasons
> smelled like — how people looked and walked

and smelled even. The memory of odors is
very rich.

    I remember that the Gabilan Mountains to
the east of the valley were light gay
mountains full of sun and loveliness and a
kind of invitation, so that you wanted to
climb into their warm foothills almost as you
want to climb into the lap of a beloved
mother.

That's John Steinbeck, summoning with incantatory
repetition the spirit of Mnemosyne to begin his epic tale
of his ancestors' Salinas Valley in *East of Eden*.

    It is through narrative that we stage time-conscious
explorations, sometimes evaluations, of remembered —
or impossible to forget — things. Here's Annie Dillard
at the opening of her scintillating memoir *An American
Childhood*:

    When everything else has gone from my
brain — the President's name, the state
capitals, the neighborhoods where I lived, and
then my own name and what it was on earth I
sought, and then at length the faces of my
friends, and finally the faces of my family —
when all this has dissolved, what will be left, I
believe, is topology: the dreaming memory of
land as it lay this way and that.

    I will see the city poured rolling down the
mountain valleys like slag, and see the city

lights sprinkled and curved around the hills'
curves, rows of bonfires winding. At sunset a
red light like housefires shines from the
narrow hillside windows; the houses' bricks
burn like glowing coals. [...]
    When the shining city, too, fades, I will see
only those forested mountains and hills, and
the way the rivers lie flat and moving among
them, and the way the low land lies wooded
among them, and the blunt mountains rise in
darkness from the rivers' banks . . .

Even when personal memory has abandoned us, even
when the reservoir of perception is emptied like a husk
from which the fruit has long since been eaten, what
remains is geological time — primordial and
impersonal landscape serving as fundament and footing
to the larger non-anthropic narrative. Story without
end.

———

LET'S LOOK AT HOW WRITERS INTERPRET, depict,
and manipulate time in their work, and to what effects.
How do writers use time, and how are they used by it?
    Another way of asking these things is: what comes
first, the events in our narrative or the narrative in our
events?

Is September 11th your birthday or that of your firstborn? Is it your wedding anniversary? Is it the date you won the lottery? Summited a mountain? Were struck by lightning? Moved into your dream house? Received your diagnosis? Lost your virginity? Laid the last stone in some great and meaningful personal pyramid? Found your faith and had your sins forgiven? Is it the date you plan to start a movement?

To a Catalan, September 11th is a day of marching and remembrance in the long push for independence.

2.

The Lips of Time

IN W.S. MERWIN'S SHORT POEM "For the Anniversary of My Death," we find a poet giving voice to the intrinsic mysteries of time, time as a carrier of fate and consequence:

> Every year without knowing it I have passed the day
> When the last fires will wave to me
> And the silence will set out
> Tireless traveler
> Like the beam of a lightless star
>
> Then I will no longer

Find myself in life as in a strange garment
Surprised at the earth
And the love of one woman
And the shamelessness of men
As today writing after three days of rain
Hearing the wren sing and the falling cease
And bowing not knowing to what

Writers have always been especially attuned to the
pressures and poignancy of time, but what I find most
remarkable about Merwin's two brief stanzas is their
quality of composure. The poem faces this essentially
brutal reality: one's round of days and dates, which
constitute one's cycle of years, adds up to only a single
transient experience within the larger collective
transience of human life. To this forlorn fact Merwin
responds not with Romantic resistance, mournfulness,
or resolve, but with a Buddhist spirit of *witness*: pure,
dispassionate, and not at all fatalistic or complacent
either. Time, in these lines, is an impassive, irreversible
force that has been going on forever and will continue
beyond us all — an inevitable force, more natural than
human life. Here we are guests of ancient time. Here it
isn't death but life itself that is the "strange garment."
And the poet's "surprise" comes not through his
realization that he will die, nor through any speculation
about nonexistence. Rather, "the earth" itself is the
surprise, as are the earthly experiences of "the love of
one woman / And the shamelessness of men."

Merwin's poem is essentially sacral in tone. For one thing, the poem intimates that time *acknowledges* us: "the last fires" will not only wave as the speaker passes into death, but will wave to him in particular ("to me"). So the universe is somehow consciously ordered, and though there is something in this order that decrees that human life must pass away, this same something is not entirely indifferent to human evanescence.

Completely unpunctuated (like much of Merwin's work), these two stanzas altogether invoke a brief but meaningful caesura in the flow of daily life. The poem doesn't call for punctuation because in itself the poem is like a single magisterial comma. The lines, in their unitary power, create a pause that is appropriate to the poem's contemplative subject: the consideration of time, of transience, and of eternity — those germane mysteries that give us all pause, or ought to, as we bow "not knowing to what."

———

Henry David Thoreau, in *Walden*, describes his own pause before the mysteries of time and existence (surprised, bowing) when he speaks of a wish "to stand on the meeting of two eternities. To toe that line." For most writers, time is a fateful presence in the mind, and a primary factor in our work and all that our work expresses, but is there any mid-nineteenth-century

American writer as time-haunted as Thoreau? (Maybe only Emily Dickinson.)

When Henry was twenty-four, his beloved brother John died in his arms — lockjaw had set in after John nicked a finger during a shave — and Henry's whole life following John's death, including his move to Walden Woods, took on new urgency and determination. "I went to the woods because I wished to live deliberately," go the famous words in *Walden*, "…and not, when I came to die, discover that I had not lived. … I wanted to live deep and suck out all the marrow of life."

Walden was first drafted in the solitude of the woods, but never without Thoreau's mental reference to the condition and outlook of his neighbors, his fellow time-passengers. In his day these were the Concord villagers. But *Walden* has proven to be an immortal book, so now it is all of us to whom this time-haunted masterpiece speaks. (It will speak to our grandchildren after us.) The author of *Walden* is a man in the same boat as you and me, and that boat is the ship of time. He may flout decorum and break the safety rules, climbing up on a handrail in his efforts to address us, but for the reader there's no mistaking this, and from the very first words we know to whom he is speaking: "I do not propose to write an ode to dejection, but to brag as lustily as chanticleer in the morning, standing on his roost, if only to wake my neighbors up."

Thoreau's project in *Walden* was to build a beacon of

metaphor amid the chaotic swirl of time, event, and his own era's increasingly disruptive technological incursions into pastoral village life: the railroad, the telegraph — both time-shattering inventions. Time, and the terms in its taxonomy, are surely the most frequent subjects of *Walden*'s sentences: "hours," "days," "seasons," "years," "ages," "ancient," "mortal"/ "immortal," "fate," "future," "dawn," and so on:

> We should live in all the ages of the world in
> an hour; ay, in all the worlds of the ages.

> I was rich, if not in money, in sunny hours
> and summer days, and spent them lavishly.

> Only that day dawns to which we are awake.

Thoreau's eponymous pond becomes a cosmic portal (for him, said Emerson, "the pond was a small ocean") as his narrative turns methodically through the seasons, compressing the author's two cabin-dwelling years into one symbolic twelve-month cycle in which time's deep layers are consistently unearthed. "Both place and time were changed," writes Thoreau midway through the book, in the chapter entitled "Where I Lived, and What I Lived For":

> I dwelt nearer to those parts of the universe
> and to those eras in history which had most

attracted me. [...] Morning brings back the heroic ages. I was as much affected by the faint hum of a mosquito making its invisible and unimaginable tour through my apartment at earliest dawn, when I was sitting with door and windows open, as I could be by any trumpet that ever sang of fame. It was Homer's requiem; itself an Illiad and Odyssey in the air, singing its own wrath and wanderings. There was something cosmical about it; a standing advertisement, till forbidden, of the everlasting vigor and fertility of the world.

Thoreau frequently invokes bygone empires and religious dynasties as he formulates his own maxims about the laws of time:

The oldest Egyptian or Hindu philosopher raised a corner of the veil from the statue of the divinity; and still the trembling robe remains raised, and I gaze upon as fresh a glory as he did, since it was I in him that was then so bold, and it is he in me that now reviews the vision. No dust has settled on that robe; no time has elapsed since that divinity was revealed.

And he casts off, deliberately and self-consciously, the paradigms by which his own nineteenth-century

New England interprets time:

> My days were not the days of the week,
> bearing the stamp of any heathen deity, nor
> were they minced into hours and fretted by
> the ticking of a clock; for I lived like the Puri
> Indians, of whom it is said that "for yesterday,
> to-day, and to-morrow they have only one
> word, and they express the variety of
> meaning by pointing backward for yesterday,
> forward for to-morrow, and overhead for the
> passing day."

———

THE SENSITIVITY AND PRESCIENCE of Merwin and Thoreau might cue this question: do writers feel time a bit more keenly than their contemporaries?

On this subject John Ruskin is especially apposite. In his conception of the powers and functions of human imagination Ruskin highlights the importance of the *not there*, including that which is not immediately at hand in the temporal sphere, and yet palpably felt:

> Now observe, while, as it penetrates into the
> nature of things, the imagination is pre-
> eminently a beholder of things *as they are*, it is,
> in its creative function, an eminent beholder
> of things *when and where* they are NOT; a
> seer, that is, in the prophetic sense, calling

'the things that are not as though they were,'
and forever delighting to dwell on that which
is not tangibly present. And its great function
being the calling forth, or back, that which is
not visible to bodily sense, it has of course
been made to take delight in the fulfillment of
its proper function, and pre-eminently to
enjoy, and spend its energy on things past
and future, or out of sight, rather than things
present, or in sight. [...] This is not a
weakness; it is one of the most glorious gifts
of the human mind, making the whole infinite
future, and imperishable past, a richer
inheritance, if faithfully inherited, than the
changeful, frail, fleeting present.*

The "changeful, frail, fleeting" days do seem to hurl
us along, as we wrestle to put the whole of our
experience into words. This hurling — and the
challenges it poses to expression — is the subject of
Dylan Thomas's poem, "The Force That Through the
Green Fuse Drives the Flower."

The force that through the green fuse drives the
flower
Drives my green age; that blasts the roots of trees
Is my destroyer.
And I am dumb to tell the crooked rose

---

* From Ruskin's *Modern Painters*

My youth is bent by the same wintry fever.

The force that drives the water through the rocks
Drives my red blood; that dries the mouthing
streams
Turns mine to wax.
And I am dumb to mouth unto my veins
How at the mountain spring the same mouth sucks.

The hand that whirls the water in the pool
Stirs the quicksand; that ropes the blowing wind
Hauls my shroud sail.
And I am dumb to tell the hanging man
How of my clay is made the hangman's lime.

The lips of time leech to the fountain head;
Love drips and gathers, but the fallen blood
Shall calm her sores.
And I am dumb to tell a weather's wind
How time has ticked a heaven round the stars.

And I am dumb to tell the lover's tomb
How at my sheet goes the same crooked worm.

Thomas, himself a doomed poet who would die at
thirty-nine, handles the same subject as Merwin here —
but could their poems be more different? Thomas's
conclusions are also quite different from Thoreau's,
although Thomas's observations are just as firmly and
rightly based in the same natural phenomena that

Thoreau observes and records. Where Merwin's lines evoke a passive and meditative acceptance ("Every year without knowing it I have passed the day..."), and Thoreau's reckoning with time is ultimately transcendental ("Time is but the stream I go a-fishing in" is his answer to the conundrum of impermanence), Thomas explores a biological/ecological realism. His poem shows human experience couched in the immutable natural laws of decay, and records the human impulse to strain against this reality. The individual's response is not, in this case, one of unqualified acceptance or surrender, but mute helplessness. "I am dumb to tell" is the inner refrain, capturing the struggle and futility of articulation in the face of this "force" that bends youth, turns blood to wax, and hauls the shroud sail. Thomas would give more ferocious expression to humanity's mortal helplessness some seventeen years later, in his poem "Do Not Go Gentle Into That Good Night," where the amplified refrain becomes "Rage, rage against the dying of the light."

In these differing poetic paradigms — Thoreau and Merwin on one side, Dylan Thomas on the other — we find an ancient dialectic in play.

————

3.

Two Ways of Looking at Time

TIME IS NOT A UNITARY, MONOLITHIC FORCE, but something various and dimensional. Time possesses different aspects and qualities, and these call for different names and symbols. *Chronos* (from which our word *chronological* derives) was the term used in classical Greece to designate what we might think of as prosaic time: the apprehensible passing of minutes, the sweep of the shadow around the sundial, that hurling sensation mentioned above. Chronos (or "Cronus," Latinized) was time as antagonist. For this reason, it would eventually take the figure of a gray-bearded man with scythe and hourglass (and sometimes a crutch). This figure, in turn, would morph into the character of the Grim Reaper. In the Roman pantheon, Cronus was Saturn, known for cannibalizing his own son (as in Goya's painting). So Chronos is time as a relentless devourer, a vanquisher.

But counterposed to Chronos was the aspect of time known to the Greeks as *Kairos.* Symbolized in Grecian art as a youthful figure, Kairos refers to an eternality found within time, a kind of permanence or significance that reposes apart from the ceaseless motion of minutes, hours, years, and centuries. It is interesting to note that Kairos holds a particular meaning as a principle of Rhetoric. As extolled by Aristotle, Kairos is the moment at which a proof is delivered. And as a more general rhetorical principle, Kairos refers to the right thing spoken at the right time (the Kairotic moment).

Italo Calvino might have been describing Kairos when he asserted, in his *Six Memos for the Next Millennium*, the power of the written word to transubstantiate time: "In practical life, time is a form of wealth with which we are stingy. In literature, time is a form of wealth to be spent at leisure and with detachment." Kairos is qualitative where Chronos is quantitative. In a sense, Kairos enfolds time. Kairos is the river itself, where Chronos is the flowing water.

It is most certainly of Kairos that Thoreau is writing in this passage from *Walden:*

> Of all the characters I have known, perhaps
> Walden wears best, and best preserves its
> purity. [...] Though the woodchoppers have
> laid bare first this shore and then that, and
> the Irish have built their sties by it, and the
> railroad has infringed on its border, and the
> ice-men have skimmed it once, it is itself
> unchanged, the same water which my
> youthful eyes fell on; all the change is in me.
> It has not acquired one permanent wrinkle
> after all its ripples. It is perenially young, and
> I may stand and see a swallow dip apparently
> to pick an insect from its surface as of yore. It
> struck me again to-night, as if I had not seen
> it almost daily for more than twenty years,—

Why, here is Walden, the same woodland lake that I discovered so many years ago; where a forest was cut down last winter another is springing up by its shore as lustily as ever; the same thought is welling up to its surface that was then; it is the same liquid joy and happiness to itself and its Maker, ay, and it *may* be to me.

We all know Chronos well, but most of us know Kairos too.

Anecdote: Hands

MANY YEARS AGO, in the special collections of the Free Public Library in Concord, Massachusetts, I sat for several hours with a thin green notebook, poring over the distinctive scrawl in its pages. A forty-five-year-old writer, sick with tuberculosis, had worked on this manuscript in his last days. At several points in the notebook his scrawl broke off, replaced by a neater, more feminine script. This was Thoreau's first draft of his essay "Walking," his prophetic final work (it would be published posthumously). Thoreau's sister and deathbed nurse, Sophia, had taken dictation when he was too weak to write.

My feelings upon holding that notebook are probably

indescribable. I was eighteen years old and I had crossed the country to Concord, alone on the longest journey of my life. I wanted to walk through the historical world of Thoreau and Emerson, the writers who meant the most to me then. I wanted to pay my respects at their gravestones. I wanted to see Walden Pond. Nothing had prepared me for the experience of turning through Thoreau's last handwritten pages — I'd had no idea such things were possible. (I still wonder what it was that compelled the special collections librarian to place that notebook in my hands. I hadn't even asked for it. I was just a kid who walked in talking about Thoreau.)

As I held them, I imagined the pages moving from hand to hand through time. First Thoreau had propped them in his lap as he sat up in his sickbed, immersed in the outpouring. Later, seeing he'd fallen asleep, Sophia slid the pages from beneath his hands — but Henry stirred and said he'd like to go on working and asked her to take down his words. The pages in Sophia's lap now, she sat beside the bed transcribing. Some days or weeks later Henry was gone, and Sophia delivered the pages to his publisher Ticknor & Fields. Years after that Mr. Fields donated the pages, bound in a green notebook, to Concord's Public Library. Then (an evaporation viewed in time-lapse) a century swirled and vanished, and there I sat in the library basement alone with those same pages, reading for hours.

My overwhelming sensation was more *spatial* than

chronological. It was as if Thoreau himself had handed me the pages across a room. And I thought, —Why, here is Henry.

The past can be held in hand. So is it truly the past? This is Kairos.

4.

Time and the Writer

THOUGH I WASN'T THINKING of the Chronos/ Kairos dialectic specifically while writing it, my first novel *The Green Age of Asher Witherow* (2004) explores themes of time, transience, and the human search for meaning and permanence. As it happens, Dylan Thomas's "The Force..." was my polestar in the writing of this book, whose title derives directly from the poem ("The force that through the green fuse drives the flower / Drives my green age..."). *The Green Age* is the story of a microcosmic empire, a short-lived coal-mining community in 19th-century California called Nortonville. The citizens of Nortonville — Welsh miners and their families — pass their doomed days in the shadow of a mountain called Mount Diablo. The narrator, Asher Witherow, is born in Nortonville in 1863 and lives there until the town's collapse some twenty-five years later. Writing in the spring of 1950, now eighty-seven years old, Asher recounts the story of those years, and as he looks back his focus is drawn constantly to the mountain as a fixed image of geological time, or what we might call Kairos. For the aged Asher this image of the mountain contrasts, in painful clarity, with the smallness and tragic Chronos of the coal-mining lives transpiring at the mountain's foot. As he relates his memory of his mother's early death in Nortonville, Asher describes a tintype taken at her casket:

> The three figures in it are pale forms, like people made of thin-worn paper. Father, long-bearded as always, stands at mother's feet, his hair oiled, one hand resting awkwardly on the rim of the casket. He looks smaller than I remember him. His face was never as diminutive and blank as that posture makes it here.
>
> I stand at mother's head, just shy of fourteen years old, nearly equal to father in height. With my frozen glance, I look prim and disinterested. Between us, mother's body runs long. Her dormant face is just as I remember it, the profile of cheek not yet fallowed by death.
>
> I look at this and can only wonder what father and I wondered then, without ever saying it. What is it that destroys? — that yellows the pages of untouched books, of drawered-up photographs? What invisible

maw digests me and my kin?

When I go to the mirror now, I stare into a
furrowed face, a mask corrugated by some
slow attrition I cannot understand, though
the process is a part of me. I have named it
age, time, entropy, but all those terms are
insufficient. It is unnamable.

Like Dylan Thomas, Asher is "dumb to tell" of time's
workings, even as they destroy and digest him.

As the novel closes, old Asher strives to assimilate
his experience of time's ruthlessness, to somehow
integrate this with the conviction he has, despite all
apparent evidence, that there is a kind of eternality to
be found somewhere within or underneath human
existence. As he describes the afternoon of his twentieth
year when he left the collapsed empire of Nortonville
for good, he muses:

Yes, all things pass, shift, lose themselves in
the memory of the earth. We already know it
to be true: we've known it for millennia. Still,
this etiology floods back to us in story after
story, pounding the shores of our collective
mind.

And yet as I walked from Nortonville up
the Somersville Rise and stood alone on that
ridge to look down again before going, I
think I was struck by an incredible sense of
permanence.

I think I saw the valley below as it would be one day: nothing but sliver and nail left of the buildings, a whole history covered in thistle and dirt, the landscape altered almost indistinguishably. And I see now what I understood in a wordless way back then: that it was a place and would always be a place, however mutable. That I would always be in that place for having been there once.

I think maybe this is my plight as an ephemeral creature. In all my temporality, I shed a kind of inexplicable residue at every moment, a substance I would know on looking back despite any alteration, for it's as elemental as nature herself. *Diagenesis* is the term the geologists use. It describes the process of sedimentation — the slow transformation of residue to rock. So my Nortonville is a faint ribbon-like stratum in the multilayered rock. So shall I be. In the meantime, of course, I'm given memory.

There is a union of Chronos and Kairos here, which is not unlike what happens in Merwin's poem:

And the silence will set out
Tireless traveler
Like the beam of a lightless star
Then I will no longer
Find myself in life as in a strange garment ...

What Asher Witherow calls "a kind of inexplicable residue" takes, for Merwin, the figuration of "the beam of a lightless star" — that is, the poet's "silence," in death, will be like a star long ago extinguished, whose light continues traveling, "tireless," into futurity. So where Asher observes, "I would always be in that place for having been there once," Merwin's realization is something like, "the silence, this silence as I hear it now, exists by virtue of my having spoken."

———

HOWEVER IMPASSIVE A WRITER MAY SEEM to be in the face of time, whether a writer's preoccupation is Chronos, Kairos, or a syncretic exploration of the two, time's presence is plain not only as subject-matter, but as *motivating force* in countless works of literature. As writers, most of us feel we're under pressure to get the words not simply written and out, but written rightly and well in the finite span allotted to us. No time, no narrative.

But that is not the whole story, just as Chronos is not the whole story, and in works of literary "experimentation" especially, we see a fuller picture.

I suspect that literary experimentation derives from the writer's keen consciousness of time — sensitivity to time's passing, yes, but also to *various times in coexistence.* This awareness opens the writer to ever-changing varieties of form, as the writer seeks new ways to express a multivalent experience of time. So the most urgently inventive literary works involve, or are primarily concerned with, time's manipulation.

5.

What's Experimental?

FIRST, THE NECESSARY DISCLAIMER: "experimental" is not a terribly accurate or useful qualifier when it comes to the literary imagination. Actually it is redundant. What we now mean by "experimental," after all, used to mean simply literature. In *Don Quixote* — the first of all western novels, published in 1605 — we find a book supremely aware of itself right from the hilarious prologue. "I can tell you," says Cervantes, "that, although it was quite an effort to write the book, producing this preface that you're now reading was far worse. Many times I picked up my pen to write it, and as many times I put it down again because I didn't know what to say..." While the author continues to bemoan the agony of creating his prologue, his "lively and clever" friend bursts into the room. Cervantes explains his predicament to this friend, elaborating about his worry that his "history" of Don Quixote will lack the customary front matter of sonnets and epigrams written by noble persons (Cervantes knows no such persons). His friend laughs him off, reassuring him point by point — and about the problem of those sonnets, says the friend, that "can be remedied if you take the trouble to write them yourself and then christen them and give them whatever names you like." This first section of *Don Quixote* winds up being the prologue that never was, but by the end Cervantes is greatly cheered, and the reader turns the page to find a lengthy section presenting those counterfeit sonnets.

The game of self-consciousness continues throughout *Don Quixote*. In chapter seven we find Cervantes's lesser characters, a barber and a priest, busily going through the knight-errant's library, discussing which books to burn. They hope to rid the madman of the cause of his madness: too much chivalric literature. They've discussed the merits or demerits of several titles when the barber picks up a new book and says, "*Galatea* by Miguel de Cervantes." The priest replies, "That fellow Cervantes has been a good friend of mine for years." In chapter nine, Cervantes abruptly breaks back into Don Quixote's "history" in the midst of a battle scene between the knight-errant and a gallant Basque. Freeze-framing his characters with their swords raised in mid-air, Cervantes informs us that this "delightful history stopped short and was left truncated, without any indication from its author about where the missing section might be found." He goes on to recount his fortuitous discovery of an Arabic manuscript in a Toledo market, and his delight in realizing that the papers continue Don Quixote's story. So the narrative may go on.

In chapter nineteen, Don Quixote speaks to his squire Sancho of "the sage whose task it is to write the history of my exploits," and explains that this writer, even then, is placing thoughts in Sancho's head and words on his tongue. In the Second Part of *Don Quixote*, Sancho and his master discuss with a young university student the existence of the manuscript we've read in Part One, and they spend four chapters commenting on its account and correcting its inaccuracies.

Would it be right to call *Don Quixote* an "experimental" work, or a "metafiction"? A spirit of experimentation — of unhindered, often playful imaginative expression — is inherent in the very origins of the novel as a literary form, and extends through its earliest practitioners: Defoe, Swift, and Sterne.

And it's not only the novel. Take *Walden:* can we call it a memoir? A nature book? A political tract? A self-help manual? A parable? A fictionalized personal history? *Walden* is all of these things, of course, and demonstrates that so-called *hybrid texts* are no newer than so-called *experimental* ones.

Time has altered our perceptions of literary "norms," and what we view today as experimentalism in literature generally represents not so much the ultra-modern as an unwitting return to the roots and foundations of this art-form.

6.

Intersections

TIME ITSELF, AS A SCIENTIFIC PHENOMENON and a direct experience, is never less than tenuous and experimental. Literature has always known this. In poetry, like music, time constitutes form as much as subject. This is also true of our most imaginative prose narratives. In literary "experiments" (so-called) we find the reversal, scrambling, subverting, or otherwise "remixing" of our conventional conceptions of chronology. The idea of time as an automatic forward motion is turned on its head or ear. Narrative time may be made to flow backward, or the narrative times of two chronological periods may be made to intersect, or multiple eras and epochs may be made to coexist in rich and bewildering collisions. Strict forward linearity is abandoned, and we are no longer resigned to the habitual complacencies or injuries of Chronos. We are startled awake.

THROUGHOUT A WRITING CAREER spanning roughly sixty years, John Berger (who died in 2017 at age ninety) was constantly engaged with the subject of time: time's presence in art, and time's effect upon our perceptions and interpretations of artistic works and also the workings of the world around us. One finds these concerns to be primary throughout his copious and wide-ranging body of writing. Berger is writing about time in his 1998 essay on the haunting Fayum portraits of first-century Egypt, when he notes that "the painted gaze [of these portraits] is entirely concentrated on the life it knows it will one day lose." He contemplates the calculated misuse of time in his famous *Ways of Seeing* (1972), which considers broadly the problem of perception in the age of the mass-produced image, and specifically the trajectory of the image from an act of artistic expression to an act of publicity: "Publicity, situated in a future continually deferred, excludes the present and so eliminates all becoming, all development. Experience is impossible within it." And time is at the forefront in Berger's unclassifiable 2005 book *Here Is Where We Meet*, which begins with the author recounting an afternoon in Lisbon in which his dead mother appears to him and then engages him in long conversation.

At the midpoint of Berger's 1995 novel *To the Wedding*, a man named Jean Ferrero finds himself in a small archeological museum in a provincial Italian town. Jean has traveled by motorbike over the mountains from his home in the south of France. He is en route to his daughter's wedding in Italy but a powerful rainstorm has compelled him to pull off the highway into this lazy backwater. He finds the doors of

the museum open, so he steps inside to take shelter
from the storm.

To the Wedding is a slim, spare novel whose
characters are spread out across southern and central
Europe. Ninon, the young bride-to-be, is in Modena,
Italy, her father will travel from Modane, France, and
her mother Zdena from Bratislava. But in telling this
small family's story, Berger invents his most gloriously
imaginative and surprisingly affecting point-of-view:
the novel's narrator is a blind Greek peddler in Athens
(Homeric echoes, yes) with a preternatural ability to *see
and listen into* the personal histories and private
moments of "strangers." The peddler can even hear/see
across the greater part of Europe to follow Ninon in
Modena, and also her scattered family members as they
journey to her wedding. This marvelous narrative
conceit enables Berger to plait together various far-
flung perceptions, and — most breathtakingly — to
leap elliptically back and forth across time. Jean
Ferrero's chance visit to the provincial museum is one
such moment.

As hail rattles down on the skylights above him, Jean
wanders through the museum gallery. He comes to a
glass display case and finds a gold necklace which dates,
as the typewritten card beside it suggests, to 1,500 B.C.

> The necklace is of golden tubes strung on a
> thread. Each tube is no longer than a child's
> fingernail is wide. After each third tube, a

beech leaf hangs from the thread, a leaf the same size as a real one. [...] And on [each leaf] veins are incised, each incision shining like a platinum hair.

Worn around the neck, the leaves would flutter against her sternum and collarbone as she walked. When she stood still, they would stir as she breathed, light and metallic, with a crisp sound. To wear this necklace would be to feel protected by every leaf of every tree in the world.

In this moment, with its shift to the conditional and imaginative — "the leaves would flutter against her sternum" — the narration steps away from the present moment into a more speculative time. Is it the future? May "she" be understood to be Jean's daughter Ninon? Or are we now in the past? Is "she" a reference to the necklace's original owner, a woman who lived 3,500 years ago?

As he stands at the display case, something overtakes Jean Ferrero. He wants to open the case. He looks for its hinges. Then he embraces the whole case and lifts. "Inside, the leaves of the necklace stir. With his arms around the case he takes several steps with the glass case against his chest."

Berger inserts a large space break, and then the Greek peddler's voice comes in, addressing us directly in the first-person:

I heard a woman's voice in Homeric Greek:
It's so long, Kallias, since you sailed. Where
are you? Come close. I undress and I take off
my necklace, my gold necklace of leaves, and
much later — after everything I choose not to
remember whilst you are away, perhaps after
we have fallen asleep once — I lie on my
back, my hair over the cushions, and I turn so
my left shoulder's in the air and my right
cheek's against the sheet, like this you are
beside me and behind me, and you lie with
your left thigh raised between my two, and it
presses upwards so I ride on it, and my right
leg I trail behind me till it finds your left calf
and, our ankles touching, we cross our two
feet and your left arm comes under mine to
hold my breast and the hand of your other
arm comes over me to hold the other one,
with your mouth on the nape of my neck and
your nose in the hollow of my occipital, like
the two of us are one, Kallias, my left hand
holding your arse … Kallias.

So from an afternoon in Europe on the cusp of a new
millennium, Berger's narrative intersects with a
moment of intense longing and privacy from millennia
past. The shift, brought on by the stirring of necklace
leaves, is not so much *across* time as *a crossing of times.*
That time and our contemporary time become, for the
duration of roughly half a page, profoundly coexistent.

And there is, in this intersection, a deeply meaningful authenticity, because the intimacy of the ancient moment reflects on the tragedy of the present one for Jean's twenty-four-year-old daughter Ninon. By this point in the novel we know, as Jean knows, that Ninon is facing an early death from AIDS. "The gift of giving myself has been taken away," she says. "If I offer myself, I offer death." Her impending wedding will be a defiantly joyful celebration, a ceremony of searing hopefulness. And simultaneously, given that this whole story originates in the imagination of that blind peddler back in Athens, the events of which we read remain suspended outside literal realism, in the timelessness of his prophetic empathy.

———

"IS IT TIME THAT TRANSLATES our lives into sequence, into meaning?" asks Ali Smith, one of our most sparklingly inventive authors, in her genre-blurring 2012 book *Artful*, an inspired mélange of fiction, essays, and criticism. "Does sequence mean that things mean? Sequence will always be most of the word consequence." *Artful* features an entire chapter entitled "On Time." Smith's equally innovative 2014 book *How to be both* is also an inquiry into the subject of time.

How does *How to be both* begin? That depends on which copy of the book you happen to acquire. This two-part novel is manufactured in dual versions. Yours could open either with a story about a mother and daughter in contemporary London, or a story narrated by the ghost of a fifteenth-century Italian painter. Smith constructs the book to make this interchangeability not only possible but thematically meaningful.

Is *How to be both* one novel or two? Is it contemporary or historical? Is it mainly philosophical or mainly narrative? Do its questions pertain to our present or to the past? At every point the answer is: both. In flowing prose, Smith puts the dualities into play from the start (whichever start you may be starting with). In one part we begin with a teenager, George, whom we learn (not immediately) is a girl. She's talking with her mother in the present-tense, but soon we read, "This conversation is happening last May, when George's mother is still alive, obviously." What seems immediate is in fact remembered, yet immediacy persists. Meanwhile, what should seem to George remote and peripheral — the work of the scarcely remembered Renaissance artist Francesco del Cossa — grows increasingly animate and important. George and her mother once went to see del Cossa's frescoes in Ferrara. "It is like everything is in layers," George reflected, as she looked with her mother's eyes at the busy paintings. "Things happen right at the front of the pictures and at the same time they continue happening, both separately and connectedly, behind, and behind that, and again behind that."

Smith sustains this layering of time, consciousness, and perspective — of life in death and death in life — throughout *How to be both*. In the book's other half her narrator is the long-dead del Cossa, whose spirit arrives in George's presence as she stands before the sole del Cossa painting in London's National Gallery. Ignored by most gallery-goers, that painting is alive yet not alive, static yet dynamic, apart from time yet subject to time's inflections, and George, by her act of seeing the painting, has unknowingly called up the artist himself. *Her*self, rather, for Smith imagines del Cossa born female and having switched genders in prepubescence in order to win apprenticeships. Smith's del Cossa is *bothness* embodied — man and woman, alive and dead, then and now. The artist's spirit trails George around, marveling as the teen manipulates her iPad, but this half of the book also succeeds, almost unthinkably, as an absorbing historical narrative evoking del Cossa's coming of age in fifteenth-century Italy.

How to be both works by anagrammatic structures and inversions, but it is never merely clever or subversive. Smith's concerns — in subject matter and form — are profound and encompassing concerns about time. It is beautiful to watch her novel refuse to be pinned to one historical or contemporary setting. After all, she seems to be saying, life is not like that.

As her del Cossa tells us, "I like very much a foot, say, or a hand, coming over the edge and over the frame into the world beyond the picture, cause a picture is a real thing in the world and this shift is a marker of this reality."

A work of literature, Smith reminds us so movingly, can be multiplicitous in all ways, especially its uses of time. Musing on his apprenticeship to master painters, del Cossa says, "I learned [...] how to tell a story, but tell it more than one way at once, and tell another underneath it up-rising through the skin of it."

———

ISN'T THIS WHAT AN IMAGINATIVE WRITER really does, irrepressibly and irreplicably? In our age of anxiety about computerized language models and the supplanting of human-made stories by machine-made ones, we must remember this.

Anecdote: Letters

WHEN I WAS TWENTY-SEVEN I went to Paris and roomed in a tiny studio apartment in the Latin Quarter while working on my second novel, *Lost Son*, about the life and work of Rainer Maria Rilke. I'd been reading Rilke since I was fourteen, and the year I arrived in Paris was my fourth year in the writing of *Lost Son*.

About midway through my time in Paris I made an appointment at the archives of the *Museé Rodin*. On the day of the appointment, I arrived promptly and had to answer only a few friendly questions before the archivist led me upstairs to a tiny garret space hidden high in the roof of the *Hôtel Biron*, home to the *Museé Rodin*.

It was Rilke who had, in 1908, first introduced Rodin to this building. The Biron was a derelict chateau in those days, but Rilke lived here off and on for a few years, working on his novel *The Notebooks of Malte Laurids Brigge*. For the footloose poet it proved to be one of his longest residences anywhere. Rodin, shortly after Rilke showed him the place, made a studio of its lofty rooms.

In the garret archives were housed perhaps a hundred letters from Rilke to his *mâitre*. The archivist brought them and I laid them out before me. Each bore the debossed tracery of the poet's pen. And instantly, as simply and easily as one might fold a dinner napkin, time turned over and I felt the palpable silence of the rooms in which the letters were written. Slow or fast, days had passed then as they do now. In his first weeks in Paris, where he had come to write a monograph on Rodin, Rilke wrote to the master: "It is not only to do a study that I have come to you — it was in order to ask you: how must one live? And you have replied: by working. And this I understand well. I sense that to work is to live without dying." That was in 1902, and during that first month in Paris, Rilke wrote in his book on the sculptor: "No strange voice came to him, no praise to confuse him, no reproach to bewilder him. ... Always his work spoke to him." Rilke was writing about himself: "Here was a task great as the world, and the one who stood looking at it was unknown by everyone; his hands reached for bread, in darkness."

———

AMIDST RILKE'S LETTERS were some receipts, some telegrams, his father's death announcement, a few of the poet's calling cards. I took up each of the calling cards in turn — those small quotidian things he'd once carried in this or that pocket. One was black-bordered. They were all very plain. Several had been jotted over with notes or messages in Rilke's hand. The center of each read simply: *Rainer Maria Rilke.* And it was as though he'd turned his face toward this future of mine and had spoken very softly, very gravely.

———

LATER, IN THE LOUVRE, that hall of gathered time, I

stood before the Archaic Torso, the subject of Rilke's celebrated poem. Moments ticked past — half an hour, hour — and slowly, I began to understand how Rilke must have waited there before that powerful object — waited, waited, and finally, confronting the torso's antique silence, felt his waiting grow fruitful. Then he knew he could give back, in words that would not profane it, the force of such silence. "Denn da ist keine Stelle, / die dicht nicht sieht. Du mußt dein Leben ändern." *For there is no piece of this that does not see you. You must change your life.*

I'd been seen by something, having stood there as Rilke did, having sat in the Hôtel Biron shuffling the poet's letters in my hands. What was it? What comes of this turning back, these travels amidst the stirring dead? How describe the experience? (T.S. Eliot: "The communication of the dead is tongued with fire beyond the language of the living.")

7.

Reversals

"IN A NOVEL THERE IS ALWAYS A CLOCK," observes E.M. Forster in his *Aspects of the Novel.* This is true, and we might add that sometimes the clock is misshapen, or melted like one of Salvador Dalí's, or turned inside-out, or set to run in a hall of mirrors, or smashed to smithereens. In the case of Martin Amis's *Time's Arrow* (1991), the clock runs strictly backward: the arrow of the title swings like a weathervane to the opposite pole.

It is no exaggeration to say that my first reading of *Time's Arrow* changed my life. The sheer authorial bravura on display was like nothing I'd known in contemporary literature. Is there another contemporary work as technically daring *and* as gracefully executed?

In structure and conceit *Time's Arrow* is potentially problematic. The novel presents a character's life lived backward not only chronologically but logistically, with people walking backward, talking backward, eating backward (and yes, *moving their bowels* backward).

> Eating is unattractive too. First I stack the clean plates in the dishwasher, which works okay, I guess, like all my other labor-saving devices, until some fat bastard shows up and traumatizes them with his tools. So far so good: then you select a soiled dish, collect some scraps from the garbage, and settle down for a short wait. Various items get gulped up into my mouth, and after skillful massage with tongue and teeth I transfer them to the plate for additional sculpture with knife and fork and spoon.

To further complicate matters, the narrator of

Time's Arrow is a separate consciousness — a kind of articulate parasite — residing within the main character's body.

> Why am I walking *backward* into the house?
> Wait. Is it dusk coming, or is it dawn? What
> is the — what is the sequence of the journey
> I'm on? What are its rules? Why are the birds
> singing so strangely? Where am I heading?
> [...] I'm powerless, and can do nothing about
> anything. I can't make myself an obsession.
>   The other people, do they have someone
> else inside them, passenger or parasite, like
> me?

As the narrative continues its dizzying rewind through the decades, from 1990s eastern U.S. to the Nazi abominations of World War II, the parasite narrator erroneously interprets the events for the reader. These include the horrors of Auschwitz, which become, through the shocking and wishful distortions of time's reversal, insanely *life*-creating.

> In the early months I still had my natural
> aversion to overcome, before I understood
> the fundamental strangeness of the process
> of fruition. Enlightenment was urged on me
> the day I saw the old Jew float to the surface
> of the deep latrine, how he splashed and
> struggled into life, and was hoisted out by

the jubilant guards, his clothes cleansed by
the mire. Then they put his beard back on.

A human born from a pool of excrement and set on
his way to increasing vigor and health: the distortion of
time yields a primordial, Darwinian stream of imagery.

> Even the most skeletal patients thrust their
> chests out for medical inspection in the last
> block on the right: a scant fifteen minutes
> earlier they were flat on the floor of the
> *Inhalationsraume*. It would be criminal — it
> would be criminal to *neglect* the opportunity
> that Auschwitz affords for the furtherance ...

The ellipsis is Amis's. Here the parasite narrator
trails off, as if buried somewhere in his conscience is a
sense, despite his ignorance, that to vouch for the value
of this place is to get things horribly wrong.

The frightful burlesque of imagery in this part of
Amis's narrative has an effect we might describe as
sickeningly hopeful: the reader is amazed to see corpses
reanimated and life restored, while simultaneously
horrified at the real sins and terrors of which we know
the Nazi guards and the main character Tod Friendly
to be guilty (he is a Nazi "doctor"). Running the
projector of the story backward to explore the
Holocaust in reverse, giving narrative and metaphorical
play to the bizarre images that arise, is the riskiest

move I've ever seen a novelist take. Yet somehow, despite its complicated morality and mechanics, the novel never gets bogged down in authorial self-consciousness or its own outlandish processes. Instead the images resonate.

The jacket of my first edition copy of *Time's Arrow* describes the book's power as "reversing the numbing effects of time and giving history the impact of direct experience." That is an apt encapsulation of the novel's success. It is also a serviceable definition of the literary technique of defamiliarization.

As articulated by the writer Viktor Shklovsky in his 1917 essay "Art As Technique," the intention behind defamiliarization is nothing less than *re-sensitization*. And it is interesting to note Shklovsky's six primary methods for achieving defamiliarization, because *Time's Arrow* uses every one of them: 1) point-of-view; 2) change of form without change of nature; 3) strange and wonderful language; 4) description of objects without naming them; 5) description of objects or events as if for the first time; 6) the disordering or attenuation of rhythm.

———

T HE WORD "NARRATE" HAS ITS ORIGINS in the Latin *narratus*, which is the plural of *narrare*, and stems from *gnarus*, or knowing, and relates to *gnoscere* or *noscere*, to know. The creative writer knows something, then, or comes to know something, and tells the story of coming to know it, or, in telling the story comes to know it. (We might reflect on the widespread misuse of the term "narrative" among televised talking heads and the chatter of the airwaves. A narrative is, by definition, a thing that makes — i.e., constructs — sense.) If this is true, and narrative relates to knowing, then to read *Time's Arrow* is to *know how we feel* — how we truly feel about events so unthinkable that our capacity to process them is constantly jeopardized.

Time's Arrow reminds me, as a writer, what art is capable of, and how infrequently — whether as artists, audience, "marketplace," or culture — we allow its potentialities to be actualized. Amis exemplifies, for me, Henry James's dictum that the novel as an art form "offers to sight so few restrictions and such innumerable opportunities." To see a writer remember and so fully actualize this fact is to be shocked awake, inspired.

8.

Collisions

TIME HAS NOT BEEN OVERLY KIND to Thornton Wilder. One of this nation's most consistently inventive and versatile authors, three-time winner of the Pulitzer Prize (twice for drama, once for fiction), and winner of the 1968 National Book Award for his epic novel *The Eighth Day*, Wilder today is usually regarded as, at best, a peripheral character in the world of American letters. Though in Wilder's own lifetime Edmund Wilson placed him (deservedly) in the company of Hemingway, Fitzgerald, and Faulkner, nowadays Wilder's dramatic masterpiece *Our Town* is hung like an anvil around his posthumous neck. Owing mostly to that play's unending overexposure in saccharine high school drama interpretations, we've all but lost the capacity to recognize the revolutionary artistry — and existential tragedy — at the heart of Wilder's best-known work. When Emily Webb, new to the afterlife, says "Goodbye to clocks ticking," she is not sentimentalizing. Rather, her words are meant to cauterize. She has learned the hard way why going back to her happiest moments is folly — why there is *never* any going back. But we can hardly hear the words of this play anymore at all, and we're all but blind to the bleak power of its bare stage. This desensitization to a playwright's major theatrical work has, in turn, cast a critical shadow over all his writing.

But now it is interesting to note, in our own apocalyptic days of climate change, global unrest, population displacement, perpetual war, and pandemic distractability, the burgeoning resurgence of Wilder's play *The Skin of Our Teeth*, which, as if it were written last week, captures all of the above (it was written in

1942). The play received a much-lauded staging at Brooklyn's Polansky Shakespeare Center a few years ago, and ran soon after in my hometown of Portland, Oregon. To see it performed is to be wonderstuck and amused by Wilder's exuberant, unflinching inventiveness, and thrilled and inspired by the vitality and relevance of the play's concerns. To sit down and read it only redoubles the effect.

The principal theme of *The Skin of Our Teeth*, much like *Our Town* and *The Eighth Day*, is time — not any single time, but universal time. But where those other works find inroads to universal time via historical specificity in their settings — Grover's Corners in 1913, or Coaltown, Illinois in 1902 — *The Skin of Our Teeth* stages an antic omnidirectional collision of *all* times. "The audience soon perceives," writes Wilder in a preface to a 1957 compendium of his plays, "that [they are] seeing 'two times at once.' The Antrobus family is living both in prehistoric times and in a New Jersey commuters' suburb of today." Wilder understates the matter. In fact, his Antrobus family is living at the beginning of an ice age, and in the time of Genesis, and in the time of Homer, and in the time of Moses, and in the time of World War II, and in the time of the final apocalypse.

The play's opening monologue, presented as a newscast, informs us of a "wall of ice" moving south across New England, and that George Antrobus, who lives with his family in a "commodius seven-room house" in that Jersey suburb, is the inventor of the wheel. And the chaotic frolic of Act One commences with the family's housekeeper Sabina fretting about the unnatural weather outside: "Here it is the middle of August and the coldest day of the year. It's simply freezing ... can anybody explain that?" By a slip of the tongue Sabina reveals that the high schooler Henry Antrobus is also the biblical Cain, responsible for his brother's death: "It certainly was an unfortunate accident, and it was very hard getting the police out of the house." With the arrival of Mrs. Antrobus, we learn that Sabina is a Sabine woman, "raped home" from her Sabine hills by Mr. Antrobus some time ago, and that there is a pesky baby dinosaur on the Antrobus's front lawn. A few pages later, taking advantage of the diversion created by a telegraph boy's arrival, the dinosaur and a mammoth slip into the house for warmth. Before long Mr. Antrobus has come home from the office. He bears under his arm the world's first wheel and boasts that today he has invented the alphabet and the number one hundred. Additional characters swarm the family's door — these are refugees seeking shelter from the ice and danger of the world outside, and we witness an all too familiar argument about what to do with them.

MRS. ANTROBUS. George, these tramps say that you asked them to come to the house. What does this mean?

Knocking at the door.

ANTROBUS. Just...uh...There are a few friends, Maggie, I met on the road. Real nice, real useful people.

MRS. ANTROBUS. *[With her]* back to the door. Now don't you ask them in! George Antrobus, not another soul comes in here over my dead body.

ANTROBUS. Maggie, there's a doctor there. Never hurts to have a good doctor in the house. We've lost a peck of children, one way and another. You can never tell when a child's throat will get stopped up. What you and I have seen—!!

He puts his fingers on his throat, and imitates diptheria.

MRS. ANTROBUS. Well, just one person then, the Doctor. The others can go right along the road.

Ultimately Mr. Antrobus wins. Despite the protestations of wife and housekeeper the doors are flung wide and the refugees are welcomed in for sandwiches. Among them, we learn, are the Nine Muses, Moses, and Homer. "The REFUGEES," say Wilder's stage directions, "are typical elderly out-of-works from the streets of New York today. JUDGE MOSES wears a skull cap. HOMER is a blind beggar with a guitar."

The driving concern of the opening act is, for the

Antrobus family, how to combat the encroaching ice and keep the fire going in their hearth. Throughout the act, Sabina repeatedly breaks the fourth wall and impedes the progress of the play with petulant outbursts: "The author hasn't made up his silly mind as to whether we're all living back in caves or in New Jersey today, and that's the way it is all the way through. Oh — why can't we have plays like we used to have..."; "I don't understand a word of this play. —Yes, I've milked the mammoth"; "Ladies and gentlemen! Don't take this play serious. The world's not coming to an end. You know it's not. People exaggerate! [...] That ice-business — why, it was a long, long time ago. Besides they were only savages. Savages don't love their families — not like we do."

Act One concludes with Sabina asking the audience to pass their chairs up to the stage for burning: "We'll need everything for this fire. Save the human race. — Ushers, will you pass the chairs up here? Thank you."

The play's second act culminates in the flooding of the earth and the Antrobus family boarding an ark (yes, together with two of every animal). The last act concerns the aftermath of a world war. And in the final transcendent moments of *The Skin of Our Teeth*, we hear from Antrobus a soliloquy on the power and supreme relevance of books — books as a living, generative force:

ANTROBUS. [...] Maggie! I didn't dare ask

you: my books! They haven't been lost, have they?

MRS. ANTROBUS. No. There are some of them right here. Kind of tattered.

ANTROBUS. Yes. —Remember, Maggie, we almost lost them once before? And when we finally did collect a few torn copies out of old cellars they ran in everyone's head like a fever. They as good as rebuilt the world.

Pauses, book in hand, and looks up.

Oh, I've never forgotten for long at a time that living is struggle. I know that every good and excellent thing in the world stands moment by moment on the razor-edge of danger and must be fought for — whether it's a field, or a home, or a country. All I ask is the chance to build new worlds and God has always given us that. And has given us

Opening the book

voices to guide us; and the memory of our mistakes to warn us. Maggie, you and I will remember in peacetime all the resolves that were so clear to us in the days of war. We've come a long ways. We've learned. We're learning.

And the steps of our journey are marked for us here.

In his preface to *Three Plays*, Wilder writes: "It is precisely the glory of the stage that it is always 'now' there," and with *The Skin of Our Teeth* he herds the chronological entirety of the human experience into this "now." The result is an effervescent work that, in whatever era it is staged, will always be both relevant and prophetic.

———

WILDER MAY GO TO EXTREMES in his use of chronological collision (and he acknowledged a debt to *Finnegan's Wake*), but he is working in a tradition that extends back at least as far as Charles Dickens's "A Christmas Carol" (1843), and can be found in the short fiction of Henry James. In James's 1908 story "The Jolly Corner" we have a narrative which, while distinctly less experimental than Wilder's play, is equally interested in the collision of disparate moments in time. An engrossing "ghost story" about ghost selves, missed opportunities, unlived lives, and paths not taken, "The Jolly Corner" is in some ways an inversion of "A Christmas Carol." Where Dickens forces an unwilling Ebenezer Scrooge to stand watching his own ghost selves, and to witness with renewed clarity the errors these selves commit, in James's main character Spencer Brydon we have a man in hot pursuit of something unrealized: a life and a self that might have been but never were.

Called back from Europe to his native New York for the first time in some thirty years in order to see to the

disposition of his childhood home, Brydon is compelled
to make decisions about real estate investments, rents,
and possible renovations. As he attends to these
necessities, it surprises him to sense a "lively stir, in a
compartment of his mind never yet penetrated, of a
capacity for business and sense for construction. These
virtues, so common all around him now, had been
dormant in his own organism." But here in New York
he finds himself "not in the least 'minding' that the
whole proposition, as they said, was vulgar and sordid,"
i.e., a matter of money only; i.e. an intrinsically
American matter. Brydon's discovery of these
unsuspected capacities within him amuses and charms
him, we are told, and he soon starts to speculate about
the life he might have led if he had never gone away to
Europe all those years ago. "What would it have made
of me, what would it have made of me?" muses Brydon,
while talking with his American friend Miss Staverton.

> "I keep forever wondering, all idiotically; as if
> I could possibly know! I see what it has made
> of dozens of others, those I meet, and it
> positively aches within me, to the point of
> exasperation, that it would have made
> something of me as well. Only I can't make
> out *what*, and the worry of it, the small rage
> of curiosity never to be satisfied, brings back
> what I remember to have felt, once or twice,
> after judging best, for reasons, to burn some

important letter unopened. I've been sorry,
I've hated it — I've never known what was in
the letter."

Miss Staverton claims to have seen his alternate self
in a dream, but when Brydon presses her for a
description of the man, she is not forthcoming. With
increasing urgency Brydon's existential questions
possess him, and he soon finds himself haunting the
empty rooms, stairwells, and corridors of his family's
old stately home, the house on its "jolly corner" of a
New York City block. Each night he comes after dark
and stays into the early morning hours, candle in hand,
pacing the rooms where his parents and siblings — all
gone now — had passed their lives in his absence. With
every such visit, he senses more and more strongly the
living presence of his own ghost-self.

He sometimes came twice in the twenty-four
hours; the moments he liked best were those
of gathering dusk, of the short autumn
twilight; this was the time of which, again and
again, he found himself hoping most. Then he
could, as seemed to him, most intimately
wander and wait, linger and listen, feel his
fine attention, never in his life before so fine,
on the pulse of the great vague place. [...]
His *alter ego* "walked" — that was the note of
his image of him, while his image of his

motive for his own odd pastime was the
desire to waylay him and meet him.

Already the pronouns are beginning to blur and
bleed together, a syntactical complexity that James will
exploit to its fullest as the eerie story progresses and
suspense mounts. So the "jolly corner" becomes a
psychological corner or cul-de-sac, a turning place of
identity, a spot ripe for the blind collision of a man's
two selves — and of two times: the man's actual time,
rendered increasingly ghost-like through his weird
wanderings, and the man's theoretical time, rendered
palpable by the summoning effect of his search.

> [He was] being definitely followed, tracked
> at a distance [...] He was kept in sight while
> remaining himself — as regards the essence
> of his position — sightless, and his only
> recourse then was in abrupt turns, rapid
> recoveries of ground. He wheeled about,
> retracing his steps, as if he might so catch in
> his face at least the stirred air of some other
> quick revolution.

Finally one night Brydon arrives at the chilling
conviction that the ghost-self is ready to face him:

> He stood in the hall and looked up the
> staircase with a certainty more intimate than
> any he had yet known. "He's *there*, at the top,

and waiting — not, as in general, falling back
for disappearance. He's holding his ground.
[...] I've hunted him till he has 'turned': that,
up there, is what has happened — he's the
fanged or the antlered animal brought at last
to bay."

Sensing this "duplication of consciousness," Brydon
steels himself and makes his way upstairs, where he
finds a shut door which — he is all but positive — was
open the last time he passed it. He draws up to the door,
listening, convinced that his every movement is being
heard. He can't bring himself to open the door. Instead,
suddenly pitying the ghost-self, he tells him, "I spare
you and I give up. [...] rest for ever, and let *me!*" He
opens a window, as if to release the trapped spirit. And
then James gives us the following lines: "He looked
again at his watch, saw what had become of his time-
values (he had taken hours for minutes — not, as in
other tense situations, minutes for hours) and the
strange air of the streets was but the weak, the sullen
flush of a dawn in which everything was still locked
up." Brydon resolves to leave the house and starts down
the stairs, but time has warped and now the prospect of
descending from the upper levels and crossing the vast
empty place to the door is almost overwhelming. At the
bottom of the stairs, he is shocked by a light from what
seems to be an open door — and then he confronts the
figure himself, apprehending every visual detail of him,

though the figure has covered his face with his hands:

> It gloomed, it loomed, it was something, it
> was somebody, the prodigy of a personal
> presence.
>   Rigid and conscious, spectral yet human, a
> man of his own substance and stature waited
> there to measure himself with his power to
> dismay. [...] Brydon, before him, took him
> in; with every fact of him now, in the higher
> light, hard and acute — his planted stillness,
> his vivid truth, his grizzled bent head and
> white masking hands, his queer actuality of
> evening-dress, of dangling double eye-glass,
> of gleaming silk lappet and white linen, of
> pearl button and gold watch-guard and
> polished shoe. No portrait by a great modern
> master could have presented him with more
> intensity, thrust him out of his frame with
> more art...

Where Dickens's tale is ultimately fabular and moral,
James's is speculative and psychological. Scrooge's
time-travel proves instructive, redemptive, and might
have been a dream. Spencer Brydon's time-collision is a
waking nightmare, confusing and frightening.
The ghost-self before him, Brydon sees, is missing two
fingers, "as if accidentally shot away," and this man,
with his minor mutilation (which seems to symbolize
his Americanism) is a stranger. "It came upon him

nearer now — the face was the face of a stranger. It came upon him nearer now [*sic*] — quite as one of those expanding fantastic images projected by the magic lantern of childhood; for the stranger, whoever he might be, evil, odious, blatant, vulgar, had advanced as for aggression, and he knew himself give ground." Scrooge, at the climax of his ghostly sojourns, confronts death. Spencer Brydon's tale rises rather to a confrontation of an alternate *self-as-death.* The Brydon he is and the maimed Brydon he might have been collide in the dim gray light of his family's grand old home. And it is here that "The Jolly Corner," if not formally experimental, constitutes a genuine experiment in the psychological manipulation of narrative time.

Finally Brydon, overcome before the figure, loses consciousness.

The story's final section serves to neatly repair the psychic splintering. It opens with Brydon awakening on the ground, his head in Alice Staverton's lap. "You came to yourself," she tells him, her words doubly significant. And she confirms that the ghost-self he describes is the same she's seen in her dreams. Through this curious clairvoyant bond, and in the relief of having come through the temporal collision of selves, Brydon sees that he loves her.

———

N ARRATIVE INTERSECTIONS AND COLLISIONS of
seemingly disparate times are more than merely
literary conceits or the product of authorial fancy.
These collisions occur in great literary works because
they occur in life. The mysteries of time are a felt
human experience that many of us know well, and it is
one of literature's vital capacities as an art form that it
can so effectively represent and explore this major facet
of our reality.*

Anecdote: Windows

O N A RAINY JULY DAY IN VIENNA, I decided to
pay a visit to one of Beethoven's apartments.
Across the boulevard from the present-day
university, three or four stark rooms are open to
visitors. They are high up on the fourth floor of a
building which itself is about four stories above street
level, having been built on a remnant of the old city
fortifications. In the first room you find a gorgeous
blonde-wood, five-pedaled piano from the composer's
day. Beyond it, on a pedestal between two windows, is
Ludwig's stern bust in bronze.

---

* Let's note that computers or "artificial intelligence,"
fundamentally insensate and powered only by "data," can never
express these undeniable mysteries of human experience the
way a living imagination can.

I moved slowly through the rooms, but found myself continually drawn back to the view from the windows in each. In the composer's time here (1804–1808), ramparts still stood where the *Ringstrasse* is today, and beyond his window he had a view of green. Nowadays the late nineteenth-century university building dominates the scene, and beyond that you see the twin spires of the massive *Votivkirche*, the Votive Church, in their neo-gothic filigree.

Out of the front windows, much closer than both of these sights, is a contemporary office building, seven or eight stories, all glass and steel. Looking at that building, you look straight into a large conference room where, on the day I visited, a man in a white shirt sat alone at the long wooden table amid seventeen empty chairs. His hands raised to the back of his head, elbows out, he was staring straight into Beethoven's apartment. We saw each other, shared an impulse to wave, then both pretended we were looking elsewhere.

———

W HILE LIVING HERE JUST OVER two hundred years ago, Beethoven worked on his fourth, fifth, seventh, and eighth symphonies, a few of the Razumovsky string quartets, and his opera "Fidelio." In two of the rooms are small stations where visitors can sit and listen through earphones to any of these pieces. Seated at one station, you look directly out the window into the windows of an eighteenth- or nineteenth-century building across the way (on the Shreyvogelgasse). In those windows, too, you can see the goings-on of a modern office, or series of offices.

With the impassioned allegro molto of the Razumovsky Quartets in my headphones, I watched a woman in profile at her desk, speaking into a telephone headset. In another window one floor above her, a man sat at his computer monitor, motionless.

Was Beethoven's time more propitious than ours, more compensatory for a dreamer who would sit listening to the sounds in his mind? No. Outside the windows, in his day too, the world went on as it will, mostly indifferent.

A few minutes later, at the neighboring station, I listened to a glorious quartet of voices accompanied by a slow set of orchestral bass tones from a section of "Fidelio" called *"Mir ist so wunderbar."*

To be in those rooms with that music in your ears is to sit for at least a few moments in Beethoven's mind and body. But my thoughts remained on those people across the street.

I hardly know what to make of these juxtapositions of time and work. The long-dead composer somehow survives in those empty rooms (if only by virtue of the many visitors who come there seeking him). His music seems to grow more and more miraculous — and more relevant. Meanwhile, in our contemporary future twenty feet away, the inexpressive workaday world ticks slowly onward for the honest employees at their desks. And sometimes, in moments of boredom or idleness, they turn — don't they? — and look across, straight into these windows, straight at the composer's ghost.

———

Whether we live in Beethoven's time or our own, we cannot always choose what we give our attention to. Time and circumstance claim us to a degree, if not totally. And yet our time and other times also coexist continually, and in some mysterious moments we can see this, vividly. It gives us pause. We stop and look. We may have thought our era stood alone in time, but now we see the spool of the future tugging steadily at our threadlike days, as it tugged at theirs.

We are not alone in time, because all times are with us.

BOOK TWO:
All times are with us.

Now I am in it. Now I am leaf
that falls in the dark of night.
Now I am tree: many-limbed
body in the blackness, past
which the big-pupiled animals
slip, crunching.

What to do with the day. What to do with the flowing
and pooling and all the images turning to bodily
impression, dream-textured in mind now the night
draws on. Be seated, sit back, and rest after roaming,
while rooms are darkened around fixtures and lamps:
this interior gloaming, and something chirruping in a
tree on the lawn. Bluebacked swallows oversoaring, and
echelons of cloud, and the boy's long legs, square
shoulders — and laughter outpouring. What to do, we
creatures whose chief attribute is our adversarial bond
with time, we who watching stayed aground against a
flight right upward where the mind and its teachers
already went. What to do but notice, what to do but
witness, what to do but await the winding light, the gold
that's never spent, what to do but wake, now and again
tomorrow, and after and always, finding the time is
right.

Rainer Maria Rilke

Ghost Coda: A Rilke Pilgrimage, or: Variations On Being Glad No One Knows You

1.

Spring, 2005

I STAND IN THE DOORWAY of the Bibliothèque
Nationale reading room, the soaring sanctum
before me, above me the ceiling a grandeur of
opaque glass wreathed with names of great cities:
Alexandria, Athens, London, Babylon, Jerusalem,
Byzantium, Peking. I'm here in search of Rainer Maria
Rilke. Strapped for cash, unschooled, twenty-seven
years old and devoid of curricula vitae save years of
assiduous reading, I've already spent an absurd,
obsessive half-decade writing a novel about him. It's
grown to more than one-hundred-fifty-thousand words.
I hope to complete it in Paris.

The roundness of this room suggests a vast egg
enclosing the world's knowledge. I want to swim forth
through the bluish light, amid the desks and along the
curving walls shelved four stories high with books, but
the clerk at the entry explains that I cannot come in. I
lack the proper license: the coveted *carte de bibliothèque*.
Malte, the main character in Rilke's single novel *The
Notebooks of Malte Laurids Brigge* (1910), cherishes the

card permitting him entrance to this room — not only for the learning the card allows him, but because the card puts an honorable seal on his otherwise dissolute life. A young scion of erstwhile aristocrats in Denmark, Malte has fled the land of his ancestry to fin de siècle Paris where he will live as a poet — or die a nobody, as his notebooks' agitated first words suggest: "So, people do come here to live. I would have sooner thought that this is where one dies." Malte's health is failing him. Destitute, squalidly housed in the Latin Quarter, he fears he's becoming indistinguishable from his neighbors: the sick, the desperate, the mad. His library card saves him, temporarily at least, from the spiritual degradation shown in those impoverished "husks of humanity" who ambulate the grim cobbled warrens around his apartment. "It is possible that one day it may occur to them to come as far as my room," writes Malte while sitting in the hush of this *salle de reference*.

> They certainly know where I live, and they
> will take care that the concierge does not stop
> them. But here, my dears, here I am safe from
> you. One must have a special card in order to
> get into this room. In this card I have the
> advantage of you ... I am among these books,
> and then taken away from you as though I had
> died, and sit and read a poet.

Discontent to remain in the doorway, I decide I must

get a card of my own. Fumbling through the necessary questions in my quasi French, I'm referred to one attendant after another. Finally, at the *Accueil*, an English-speaking clerk directs me across the library's palatial foyer to the enclosed area marked "Orientation des Lecteurs." Bureaucracy-phobes acquire nightmares here.

Wound up and out of sorts, I breach the shrine and install myself in a chair before a librarian's desk, babbling. Gatekeepers make me nervous. And now I'm much too aware, in my tongue-tied foreignness, in my pullover and backpack and scuffed sneakers, that I cut the figure of a failed pretender, a would-be tourist-cum-scholar. Worse, I give the impression, despite myself, of knowing my own charade, knowing I cannot claim legitimate candidacy for the access I seek. The library wardens — officious, serious, and thoroughly French in their skeptical decorum — reduce me with every sidelong glance. They won't grant a card to just anybody. As my stuttering interview concludes, I'm instructed to return with passport and proof official of my status as an author; e.g., a published book. I will thereafter be informed of materials in the library relevant to my research.

Rattled, I exit the marbled lobby, cross the cobbled courtyard to the ravine-like rue de Richelieu, and start back toward my cramped studio apartment on the Left Bank. As I walk I pocket my clammy hands and replay the interview. Did I call myself *un écrivain* or *romancier*?

Which was more correct considering my motive? I know I said *recherche* — that was a kind of lie. But how can I explain that I've got nothing to research, at least not in the manner they mean? How explain that I simply wish to sit and work in that reading room, that the spirit of the room itself is what I'm after?

A Vespa skirls past, the rider's shadow splayed like the covers of an open book, half on sidewalk half on stone wall. The green dome of the Ópera swells beyond the buildings ahead, the sun shafting low along its bulge. The river, when I cross the Pont du Carrousel, will be a blinding glare. I'm not sure whether I'll follow through on today's attempt. I do have a published book, but for some reason I demur to brandish it like a business card. "*Merci, mais non,*" they could say, dismissing book and boy with a wave of the hand.

———

ARRIVING HERE IN HIS DISTURBED AUTUMN of 1902, applying to the library wardens behind their imposing desks, twenty-six-year-old Rilke himself probably worried they'd deem him ineligible. He'd likely rehearsed the process in his head, working out the French phrases (he was far from fluent yet). He would explain that he meant to do research about their great sculptor Rodin — this was true, he was writing a monograph, a commission for which he'd left his wife and small daughter at home in the north of Germany. But he probably felt the stony dusk of the foyer reducing him, and he knew he lacked the brio of a credible academic. Thank God, then, that his publisher had supplied him a letter. This letter would render his intentions official, it would work like ersatz confidence, he could brandish it and let it be his brio.

How would Rilke have comported himself in the absence of a letter? It's important, from this obscure future of mine, to wonder such things. I was intimidated, to be sure. But as Rilke's own work attests — as *Malte* demonstrates — a sufficient sense of helplessness can return one powerfully to one's beginnings, and for an artist this is proper. Exposed and vulnerable, one avoids a numbing insularity. One senses the world anew. If the library personnel have sensitized me to my status as an unapproved, unaffiliated outsider, they've done me a peculiar service. A few words from Rilke's *Letters on Cezanne* ring in my head, a fine affirmation for just such a moment: "One has to be able at every moment to place one's hand on the earth like the first human being."

———

RAINER MARIA RILKE STROVE unceasingly to wrest poetic creation from experience, "to see in everything I encounter a challenge, a task, a claim to artistic transformation."* That was his drastic lifelong vow, made early on and relentlessly fulfilled, so that this *everything* included even Rilke's final experience, his death. In Switzerland in 1926, as his last bleak hours steepened with pain, he barred his door and refused all visitors. Not even his wife Clara was admitted, for Rilke had pledged himself to this, if death was what it was; he would embrace it without intermediary. He was fifty-one. For weeks he'd writhed with what his physician would call leukemia, but Rilke allowed no one to tell him the name of the disease undoing him. In striving to confront his fate, to *create* by unmediated perception that last experience, he refused all medicine. If it was torment, it would be his own — not the doctor's, not the disease's. Unnamed, pure, and purely awful, it would be *his* death, a thing achieved, a thing as suited to him as his birth and no less singular. What else, as Rilke saw it, could being a poet mean? What, but to begin and begin, to remain endangered, to embrace one's honorable obscurity and accept its absence of reward, to reconcile oneself to life's mortal loneliness, to nurture one's vision in that solitude and sing? Art, as Rilke wrote to the young poet Franz Xaver Kappus in July of 1903, "means loving one's solitude and bearing its pain by making beautiful sounds of one's complaint."

"Young person anywhere, in whom something is rising up that causes you to shiver," says Malte Laurids

* From Rilke's letter to Ellen Key, 9 October 1908

Brigge, "make use of the fact that no one knows you. ...
Beg no one to speak of you, not even contemptuously."
Though the protagonist pens them, these words belong
as rightly to the author himself. One of the great self-
chroniclers of all time, Rilke dispatched more than
eleven thousand letters over the course of thirty-five
footloose years. This correspondence rehearses the story
of his life, stringing the narrative onto an armature of a
few key episodes, obsessively testifying to their
importance. They include: Rilke's mother rearing him as
a girl following the death of an infant daughter prior to
his birth; that mother's inculcation of a superstitious
spirituality in the boy, accounting for the poet's lifelong
sensitivity to ghosts and the subharmonic vibrations of
the paranormal; a young and sickly René Maria (as the
pious mother christened him) suffering five miserable
years of military boarding school; the poet's artistic
coming-of-age under the influence of Lou Andreas-
Salomé (lover, Madonna, muse); the poet's reverence
before his Master, Auguste Rodin, who became idol and
surrogate father in one. From unpromising beginnings
through his ongoing tribulations of homelessness and
alienation, adoration and heartbreak, his incapacity to be
loved, his brushes with incandescent beauty, the letters
chronicle everything important to the poet, all
experienced in the name of art. Rilke presented to the
world the persona of the unadulterated artist committed
wholly and exclusively, at every living hour, to his work
— and committed no less to that work's frequent

lacunae in which, semi-religiously, he strove to "be inactive with confidence." As he wrote to an aggrieved Clara in 1906, amid years of separation for the sake of this work, "I am absolutely determined to miss none of these voices which are to come. I want to hear each one."

For some today, Rilke is a figure of saintly poetic renunciation offering, as translator Anita Barrows puts it, "instructions for living." Others denounce him as a profligate husband and father. Among the fault-finders, poet John Berryman's verdict is gleefully fetishized: "Rilke was a jerk." "Lap dog" also recurs, a favorite epithet for this poet who lived in — and thanks to — a bygone age of patronage. In a *Time* Magazine article of 1941, Rilke is "a lap dog for cultivated ladies, loveless as a serpent, soaked to the soul in the most indecent self-pity." Garrison Keillor dutifully took up this theme in his commemoration of the poet on National Public Radio's "The Writer's Almanac" in 2006:

> Since [Rilke] only wrote in spurts, he supported himself by getting rich noblewomen to fall in love with him and support his work. He apparently wasn't the best-looking guy in the world, but women found him irresistible because he was so romantic and poetic.

Is there narcissism in Rilke? Naturally, perhaps necessarily so. But nefariousness? Only a kneejerk cynicism can lead to such a conclusion. Canonizers and attackers aside, the murk of an actual life will rarely distill smoothly to a thesis statement, and the truth is that Rilke's life is stubbornly less tidy than his worshippers might wish, and stubbornly less diabolical than alleged by those who would retroactively police his morality.

In a 1960 introduction to the poet's selected letters, editor Harry T. Moore observed, "Those who knew Rilke have never blamed him for following the necessities of his poetical nature: if he sometimes avoided everyday obvious reality, he constantly sought a deeper reality." Bravely, Moore added: "Those who criticize his conduct couldn't have written his poetry." Rilke's naysayers might more clearly bear in mind the nature of the man and his work, and avoid projecting onto him standards of artistry or comportment to which he never pledged himself. Rilke was no Whitmanesque adorer of everyman or celebrant of the commonplace. His poetry, while in some places extolling a spiritual interconnectedness, did not draw him out of doors or out of himself into warm-spirited intercourse with his siblings among the children of the world. He was not disposed to comfort battle-wounded youths in hospital wards or rub elbows with brethren urbanites on joyous omnibus excursions. Instead, Rilke's self-proclaimed "calling" led him away from the common life — and yes, the familial constraints, quotidian inspirations, and proletarian sentiments such living might include.

Knowing how ill-suited he was to be the object of any binding affections (a major theme of *Malte*), Rilke leapt into what, by most contemporary pragmatic rationales (particularly American ones), can only be viewed as an existence shamelessly self-indulgent (read: dreamy and unpaid). Ultimately, for Rilke art was a way of life. For art's sake he cultivated a kind of purist bohemianism, an unrelenting pursuit of the conditions propitious to creation. Solitude was a crucial ingredient, penury a byproduct (he was never a breadwinner). Rilke's yearning prayer he borrowed from Baudelaire, impassioned defender of "illustrious unfortunates": "Lord God, grant me the grace to produce a few beautiful lines." And Rilke's modus operandi he borrowed from Rodin: "One must work. Nothing but work!" He needed his art to be all-consuming. As for friends and family, they understood him. Why don't we? Is it largely because we cannot imagine being an artist *and* glad that no one knows us? Because today we equate anonymity and obscurity with failure and shame? Had Rilke been more intent on establishing his "platform," would we better understand?

———

2.

DESPITE MY FEARS, they've let me in. Maybe I encouraged them to believe I had scholarly aims, or did nothing to dispel the impression. Anyway, I've been vetted and my one book has spoken for me. What a marvel that was after all: to have a book to show them. And now, like the poet's brainchild and second self, Malte Laurids Brigge, and like Rilke before him, I may sit in this grand room and read.

> There are now perhaps three hundred people
> in the hall, reading. But it is impossible that
> each and every one has a poet (God knows
> what they have). Three hundred poets there
> are not. But see now — how's this for destiny
> — I, perhaps the most dejected of these
> readers, a foreigner: I have a poet. Even
> though I am poor.

Here at hand lies my hard-won Bibliothèque Nationale researcher's card. The rectangle of yellow plastic bears a tiny color photograph taken at my interview and reproduced instantaneously by computer. What a weirdly stern image: the guarded face of one prepared to prove himself — though by the time this little portrait was made the greatest trial, the trial of explaining my intentions (in halting French), was already over. They'd decided to let me in, and my submitting to their camera was a formality no different than plunking down their researcher fee (4.50 euro).

How do you explain yourself, you who harbor dreams but have no means to certify them for others? — you who remain outside, absent, unknown and poor? — you whose future is always in question (if not in danger)? Maybe I've sought access to this monumental reading room merely to explore these dilemmas. Where are the *salles de sanctuaire* or by-admittance-only zones for one who lacks this or that institution's card? — lonely one dressed again in yesterday's clothing, you who have no name and carry no credentials, you whose cuffs are fraying like Malte's, unsung one who strives to sing.

And Rilke, what can we expect our world to do with you? Intellectual Marjorie Perloff, in a 2000 essay in *Parnassus*, broods doubtfully upon your legacy: "Can anyone living at the turn of the twenty-first century really believe that Art somehow redeems life, that it has no political or ethical obligations?" What were your friends and family to do with you, Rilke? In my book about you, which I will manage to finish some years later, I'll ask as much:

> What is the world to do ... with one who
> travels endlessly and sleeps in an unshared
> bed and takes long walks alone and sits at a
> desk and works and waits in order to simply
> say something, not even to name something
> but just to take the name already possessed
> and say it over again, to show it, show it, hold
> it up in two devout hands in its beauty or
> splendor or fright, and in this way give back
> to maybe one person (maybe no more than
> one) the wondrous disquiet this person once
> knew as a child when first faced by the thing
> they're now seeing again. In your Ninth *Duino
> Elegy*, Rilke, you expressed this yourself:

>> "To say — understand this now —
>> oh to say these things
>> in such a way
>> that the things themselves would never
>> have thought to exist so earnestly."

Even now I'm worried I might be found out — that the librarians will discover I'm guilty of wanting so little, wanting to just sit here and think on these things and see how such thoughts may change and help one who hopes to create.

There is no monument in this room. But once, a young foreigner, a threadbare poet of twenty-six, was given leave to linger amidst these storied bookstacks ("Probably the most extensive in the world" says the 1902 Baedecker of this Bibliothéque). How does that change a place? What memory can an airy library hold of a young nobody's fierce, secret, silent inspirations?

In his time here Rilke read Baudelaire, Flaubert, and a poet called Francis Jammes, but I am reading Rilke. My dog-eared English copy of his wonderful, terrible novel lies open before me. If the book were an eye, it would see me bent in an elliptical field of light, and encircling my skull like a crown of thoughts the names of cities as they're inscribed overhead: *Berlin, Alexandrie, Londres, Babylone, Vienne, Thebes, Rome.* I sit here and read Rilke in this room where he read his poet, and I feel my poverty, my obscurity, flowing on and on down the ages.

3.

I N THE DAYS FOLLOWING MY PILGRIMAGE to the Bibliothèque Nationale, I use my newfound fortitude to make an appointment at the Auguste

Rodin archives. Appearing promptly at the scheduled hour, I have to answer only a few friendly questions (a relief). The archivist leads me upstairs to a tiny garret space hidden high in the roof of the Hôtel Biron, home to the Museé Rodin. The Biron was a derelict chateau when Rilke lived here. He stayed off and on for a few years, working on *Malte*. It was one of his longest residences anywhere. Rodin, shortly after the poet showed him the place, made a studio of its lofty rooms. In the garret are housed perhaps a hundred letters from Rilke to the sculptor, his *mâitre*. The archivist brings them and I lay them out before me. Each bears the debossed tracery of the poet's pen.

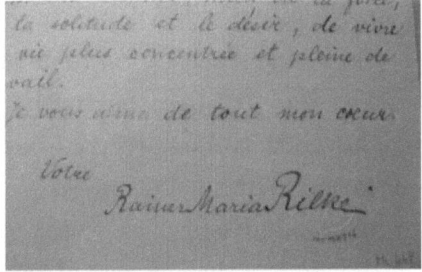

And instantly, as simply and easily as one might fold a dinner napkin, time turns over and I feel the palpable silence of the rooms in which these lines were written.

Slow or fast, days passed then as they do now. In his first weeks in Paris, Rilke wrote to Rodin:

It is not only to do a study that I have come to

you — it was in order to ask you: how must
one live? And you have replied: by working.
And this I understand well. I sense that to
work is to live without dying.

During that first month in Paris, he wrote in his book
on the sculptor: "No strange voice came to him, no
praise to confuse him, no reproach to bewilder him. ...
Always his work spoke to him." Rilke was writing about
himself: "Here was a task great as the world, and the one
who stood looking at it was unknown by everyone; his
hands reached for bread, in darkness."

Later, in the Louvre, that hall of gathered time, I will
stand before the Archaic Torso, the subject of Rilke's
celebrated poem. Moments will tick past — half an
hour, hour — and slowly, I will begin to understand
how Rilke must have waited there before that powerful
object — waited, waited, and finally, confronting the
torso's antique silence, felt his waiting grow fruitful.
Then he knew he could give back, in words that would
not profane it, the force of such silence: "Denn da ist
keine Stelle, / die dicht nicht sieht. Du mußt dein Leben
ändern." *For there is no piece of this that does not see you.*
You must change your life.

I've been seen by something, having bent my head in
the reading room, having shuffled the poet's letters in
my hands. What is it? What comes of this turning back,
these travels amongst the stirring dead? How describe
the experience? (T.S. Eliot: "The communication of the

dead is tongued with fire beyond the language of the living.")

As Rilke did, I need to understand my position, my part, my values in this time, to ask: How am I to live? How work? We all need to know. Retracing his steps, decoding his letters, I do not query Rilke so much as myself. And yet I see, also, that at the center of these questions lies something much larger than me and my particular life. If your work has no roof to shelter it, find the roof inside you: often it's an arch of words, the good words that arch when you're reading.

Whoever I am, whatever *my* name may be, is unimportant. Young person anywhere, clasp your hands and say this. Be glad that no one hears you say it, and if you notice your cuffs are fraying, don't worry — say it anyway. Only the inkling, the idea is important, and the pilgrimage of thought that leads there, where there is no place for judgment, only the allure of ghosts, only the learning-to-be-haunted, which some call inspiration.

Always, John

In Memoriam, John Berger 1926–2017

O NE SPRING SOME YEARS AGO, by the good
graces of mutual friends, a small parcel
traveled from my home in Portland, Oregon
to John Berger's home in France. Included in the parcel
was a brief letter:

> Because I have read, admired, and drawn
> immense inspiration from your work for many
> years now, I feel I have simply too much to
> say to you — and hardly know where to start
> — so I will let the enclosed book do the
> saying, mostly. ... There are some few
> glistening gossamer threads linking this work
> to yours. Without those strong fibers, I'm not
> sure the book would ever have been imagined.

That book was *Partisans*, a philosophical novel in
which Janos Lavin, the main character from John's own
debut novel *A Painter of Our Time* (1959), is referenced
as a real artist. But that's just one point of connection.
John's body of work inspires *Partisans* throughout and I
wanted him to know this. Since I'd published *Partisans*
myself in samizdat fashion — there would be no

promotion and no reviews — he would only know if I told him.

At first I wasn't sure how to address my letter. We'd never met, but "Mr. Berger" wasn't right, nor was "Dear John." After much thought, I settled on "Dear John Berger." It felt most natural, finally, to rely on the name's printed incarnation, the name as it appeared in all those books I'd been reading for so long.

John's reply arrived a few weeks later, a handwritten note in a small white envelope. He'd signed himself "Always, John." That's how I think of him now, so that's how I write of him here.

———

ON BRITISH TELEVISION IN 1972, standing in a room of the National Gallery, John reached up with a knife and cut into a Botticelli. He removed the cut-away square of canvas, the head of Venus now disjoined from the luxuriant atmosphere of the larger painting where she'd lounged with Mars amid rampant cherubim.

The camera then showed a printing press in action, the head of Venus copied again and again by machine. And now the viewer understood the room, the canvas, and the Venus as reproductions.

This was the opening of the revolutionary *Ways of Seeing* series, much of which was filmed in the actual National Gallery.

"Reproduction," John would write in the accompanying book, "isolates a detail of the painting from the whole. The detail is transformed. An allegorical figure becomes a portrait of a girl." He was telling us what he would express elsewhere, some years later, in these ways:

> With the loss of memory the continuities of meaning and judgment are also lost to us. The camera relieves us of the burden of memory. It surveys us like God, and it surveys for us. Yet no other god has been so cynical, for the camera records in order to forget. ("Uses of Photography," in *About Looking*)

> The first step toward building an alternative world has to be a refusal of the world-picture implanted in our minds and all the false promises used everywhere to justify and idealize the delinquent and insatiable need to sell. ("Against the Great Defeat of the World," in *The Shape of a Pocket*)

———

T HIRTY-SIX YEARS AFTER *WAYS OF SEEING*, on Good Friday 2008, John stood in a different room of the National Gallery, age 82 now, sketching Antonello da Messina's painting of the crucifixion. An armed security guard, finding John's shoulder bag placed in an empty attendant's chair, reprimanded him. John moved the bag to the floor between his own feet, but the guard demanded that he pick it up and wear it. John tried to go on sketching, but the guard grew more insistent. A confrontation began which lasted several minutes. Then two security guards bustled John to the gallery entrance and out onto the sidewalk.

"Memory implies a certain act of redemption," John had written in 1978. "What is remembered has been saved from nothingness. What is forgotten has been abandoned. If all events are seen, instantaneously, outside time, by a supernatural eye, the distinction between remembering and forgetting is transformed into an act of judgment, into the rendering of justice, whereby recognition is close to *being remembered*, and condemnation is close to *being forgotten*." ("Uses of Photography")

Memory, justice, silence, human compassion, the act of seeing, resistance, subversion, the restoration of the natural, communal, and sustainable — all were primary concerns in John's essays and fiction.

In his 1995 novel *To the Wedding*, John invented his most gloriously imaginative and affecting narrator: a blind Greek peddler in Athens (Homeric echoes, yes) whose sensitivity to the passing voices of strangers enables him to see and listen into their personal histories and private moments, even to hear/see across the greater part of Europe to follow a few scattered members of a family as they journey to a wedding.

Early on the narrator explicitly informs us, "Blindness is like the cinema, because its eyes are not either side of a nose but wherever the story demands." This touches on something far more subtle and suggestive than the tired 'narration as camera' analogy used with regard to fiction writing. Rather than the novelist pointing the 'lens' of his own narration here and there like an authorial movie camera, by giving us the intermediate consciousness of the blind Greek man John gives his story an expansiveness, a mysteriousness, a dimensionality of the kind that only fiction can give (and film and filmic conventions cannot).

Here's a small passage:

> The motorbike with its headlight zigzags up the mountain. From time to time it disappears behind escarpments and rocks and all the while it is climbing and becoming smaller. Now its light is flickering like the flame of a small votive candle against an immense face of stone.
>
> For him it's different. He is burrowing through the darkness like a mole through the earth, the beam of his light boring the tunnel and the tunnel twisting as the road turns to avoid boulders and to climb. When he turns his head to glance back — as he has just done — there is nothing except his taillight and an immense darkness.

Having *listened his way into* the story of Jean Ferrero as Jean rides his motorbike from the south of France over the mountains to his daughter's wedding in Italy, the blind narrator, back in Athens, finally *sees* the lone rider from all levels: from high up against the greater landscape, from Jean's very seat astride the motorcycle, and finally from within Jean's own eyes. And what is so strangely moving about this unorthodox point-of-view is its person-to-person basis. Here, instead of an omniscient authorial presence overseeing the lives and destinies of his minion characters, the reader finds a humble blind man whose sensitivity and attunement becomes exemplary. *We notice more keenly the blind man's act of noticing and imagining* than we would an author's, because he seems to have no controlling interest. His stake in the story is pure. And we, in turn, want to listen and see and imagine as purely as he does. In other words, we want to care. And so we do: we enter the novel and we care. But somehow, too, when the story has ended, we bring that caring out of the book with us and apply it anew to the world.

The book itself embodies and teaches compassion. In an essay on Géricault's portrait of a man with tousled hair (a painting from a series Géricault made in a Parisian insane asylum), John marvels at the artist's clarity, pity, and compassion:

> ... A compassion which refutes indifference and is irreconcilable with any easy hope. ...

Compassion has no place in the natural order of the world, which operates on the basis of necessity. The laws of necessity are as unexceptional as the laws of gravitation. The human faculty of compassion opposes this order and is therefore best thought of as being in some way supernatural. To forget oneself, however briefly, to identify with a stranger to the point of fully recognizing her or him, is to defy necessity, and in this defiance, even if small and quiet and even if measuring only 60 cm. x 50 cm., there is a power which cannot be measured by the limits of the natural order. It is not a means and it has no end. ("A Man with Tousled Hair," in *The Shape of a Pocket*)

———

"THANK YOU," I WROTE TO JOHN IN MY LETTER, "for your novels, stories, poems, essays, and studies — and the clear sight and uncompromising spirit your work always exemplifies."

In the parcel I'd also enclosed a copy of remarks I'd made a few days before, while introducing *Partisans* in a small public event at Powell's Books. *It's fitting*, I'd said to the ten or twelve people present that night, *that we gather in this secret place, among real books, beyond the digital eye of the Network and the Market Optimization Bureau. Coming together here is a significant act of resistance.*

The future is upon us, and we need to stick together in these times — and in the times ahead. Tonight we remind ourselves of this because one of our own, one who went missing some time ago, has left us a manuscript.

I went on (to the mystification of some present) to speak of Geoffrey Peerson Leed, the disappeared author whose manuscript I had shaped into *Partisans: One can learn a great deal about G.P. Leed — about his uncomfortable place in this future of ours — from reading his strange manuscript; I certainly have. But there is still a vast amount of things we cannot know, and nowhere in the rest of the archive are these questions answered. Who exactly was he? Where was he born? What was his childhood like? His homelife? What did he look like? How did he become the kind of writer he was? What were the exact circumstances of his disappearance? All questions without answers. But we have Partisans, and as we read it I think we come to feel that these specific things, these lacunae and redacted parts, are not so important. What matters and will continue to matter is the spirit of the man, the resolve he displayed in the face of all that opposed the work he was doing ...*

"There are two categories of storytelling," John writes,

> those that treat of the invisible and hidden, and those that expose and offer the revealed. What I call — in my own special and physical sense of the terms — the introverted category and the extroverted one. Which of the two is likely

to be more adapted to, more trenchant about
what is happening in the world today? I
believe the first.

Because its stories remain unfinished. Because
they involve sharing. Because in their telling a
body refers as much to a body of people as to
an individual. Because for them mystery is not
something to be solved but to be carried.
Because, although they may deal with sudden
violence or loss or anger, they are long-
sighted. And, above all, because their
protagonists are not performers but survivors.
(*Bento's Sketchbook*)

———

I AM REREADING HIS WORK THIS MORNING, as I've done
so often before. Inevitably the inflections are different
now that he's gone — but the force of his inspiration
only grows.
    On the consolations of seeing:

In art museums we come upon the visible of
other periods and it offers us company. We
feel less alone in face of what we ourselves see
each day appearing and disappearing. So
much continues to look the same: teeth,
hands, the sun, women's legs, fish ... in the

realm of the visible all epochs coexist and are fraternal, whether separated by centuries or millennia. ("Step Towards a Small Theory of the Visible," in *The Shape of a Pocket*)

On Van Gogh:

I can think of no other European painter whose work expresses such a stripped respect for everyday things without elevating them, in some way, without referring to salvation by way of an ideal which the things embody or serve. Chardin, de la Tour, Courbet, Monet, de Staël, Miró, Jasper Johns — to name but a few — were magisterially sustained by pictorial ideologies, whereas he, as soon as he abandoned his first vocation as a preacher, abandoned all ideology. He became strictly existential, ideologically naked. The chair is a chair, not a throne. The boots have been worn by walking. The sunflowers are plants, not constellations. The postman delivers letters. The irises will die. And from this nakedness of his, which his contemporaries saw as naivety or madness, came his capacity to love, suddenly and at any moment, what he saw in front of him. ...

As he sits with his back to the monastery looking at the trees, the olive grove seems to close the gap and to press itself against him.

He recognizes the sensation — he has often experienced it, indoors, outdoors, in the Borinage, in Paris or here in Provence. To this pressing — which was perhaps the only sustained intimate love he knew in his lifetime — he responds with incredible speed and the utmost attention. Everything his eye sees, he fingers. And the light falls on the touches on the vellum paper just as it falls on the pebbles at his feet — on one of which (on the paper) he will write Vincent. ("Vincent," in *The Shape of a Pocket*)

On pain and resistance:

That she became a world legend is in part due to the fact that in the dark age in which we are living under a new world order, the sharing of pain is one of the essential preconditions for a refinding of dignity and hope. Much pain is unshareable. But the will to share pain is shareable. And from that inevitably inadequate sharing comes a resistance. ("Frida Kahlo," in *The Shape of a Pocket*)

On the language and effect of poems:

Poems, even when narrative, do not resemble stories. All stories are about battles, of one kind or another, which end in victory and defeat. Everything moves towards the end, when the outcome will be known.

Poems, regardless of any outcome, cross the battlefields, tending the wounded, listening to the wild monologues of the triumphant or the fearful. They bring a kind of peace. Not by anaesthesia or easy reassurance, but by recognition and the promise that what has been experienced cannot disappear as if it had never been. Yet the promise is not of a monument. (Who, still on a battlefield, wants monuments?) The promise is that language has acknowledged, has given shelter, to the experience which demanded, which cried out.

Poems are nearer to prayers than to stories, but in poetry there is no one behind the language being prayed to. It is the language itself which has to hear and acknowledge. For the religious poet the Word is the first attribute of God. In all poetry words are a presence before they are a means of communication. (*And Our Faces, My Heart, Brief as Photos*)

On creating:

You put something down and you don't immediately know what it is. It has always been like that. ... All you have to know is whether you're lying or whether you're telling the truth, you can't afford to make a mistake about that distinction any longer. (*Here Is Where We Meet*)

———

I SOMETIMES THOUGHT I'D WRITE HIM a second letter — and maybe a third. My main impulse was to further express my thanks. I knew he was getting old, I'd heard something about his health concerns, but by all remote appearances he seemed as productive, alert, and articulate as ever. Surely there'd be plenty of time, and I felt certain he'd respond. Clearly he was generous that way. In just the few brief lines with which he replied to my parcel, John transmitted such humanity, such humility and understanding warmth, that I had no doubt he'd *taken me in*, that he would remember me now.

Accept the unknown. There are no secondary characters. Each one is silhouetted against the sky. All have the same stature. Within a given story some simply occupy more space. (*Bento's Sketchbook*)

On the verso of the page in the book where these words appear, I find John's portrait of the person who helped me contact him, another generous spirit whom

I'd never met. The portrait is luminous. It still surprises me with joy.

How many people did John touch directly with that magnanimity, that same clarity of vision and heart that infuses his work?

In reply to what I sent him John wrote, at 89 years and in poor health, an expression of genuine gratitude: *Thank you so much for writing to me. Your letter was a great encouragement. It offered me energy.*

> Dear Mark,
> Thank you so much for
> writing to me . Your letter was
> a great encouragement . It offered
> me energy .

Encouragement. Energy.

> The stakes were high, the margin narrow. And in art these are the conditions which make for energy. ("The Fayum Portraits," in *The Shape of a Pocket*)

Why do we reach out to those we admire? If I'd hoped for a benediction, a godspeed, John offered back something even greater. He showed me that I'd helped *him* in some way I couldn't have expected. That was a profound gift.

He said: *And thank you for Partisans, where we'll join forces.*

And he wrote: *We continue, yes? Yes.*

We continue , yes ? Yes .

————

A presence, a visible presence, is sometimes most eloquently conveyed by a disappearance.

Who does not know what it is like to go with a friend to a railway station and then to watch the train take them away? As you walk along the platform back into the city, the person who has just gone is often more there, more totally there, than when you embraced them before they climbed onto the train. When we embrace to say goodbye, maybe we do it for this reason — to take into our arms what we want to keep when they've gone. ("Will It Be a Likeness?" in *The Shape of a Pocket*)

My reading this morning is my embrace. Thank you again, John. Yes. We continue.

Variations on the Now

(2009 - 2013)

Civics

Trying to define civilization in his TV series of the same name, Kenneth Clark quotes John Ruskin: "Great nations write their autobiographies in three manuscripts, the book of their deeds, the book of their words, and the book of their art. Not one of these books can be understood unless we read the two others, but of the three the only trustworthy one is the last."

Clark continues, in his own words: "Civilization requires a modicum of material prosperity — enough to provide a little leisure. But, far more, it requires confidence — confidence in the society in which one lives, belief in its philosophy, belief in its laws, and confidence in one's own mental powers."

———

Try this theory against observation. What evidence, living here, living now, and looking about, can one find of these things? *Confidence? ... Belief? ...*

Screen

NECESSARY TO CONSIDER the degenerative influence and force of the Internet. The "decentralized" behaviors it promotes tend to undermine an age-old emphasis on the importance of municipal (geographical) citadels of knowledge and human achievement. The importance, that is, of *civilizational centers* of the real and local kind. Therefore: the newly lost emphasis on pride of civic life, civic aspiration, city as beacon, local culture as exemplary, etc. The loss ultimately (but we are still some distance from this point, thankfully) of an infrastructure that is more than barely functional.

———

THE MONEY-FLAUNTING CITIES orbiting Silicon Valley: the problem is palpable there. The pride one finds inside the cities of Silicon Valley is the pride of the very few, a pride of the kind that can only result in the betterment of those few, all too often at the detriment of the many. To enrich oneself beyond all reasonable proportion through one's service to "web culture" and to all the technocratic idealism (ideology) that goes with it — how can the collective benefits borne of this (if any) compare to a commitment to sound transit infrastructure, to quality of life through the preservation of open spaces, investment in libraries, development of thriving, dynamic, pluralistic, and inviting city centers, &c., &c.?

———

GEORGE SANTAYANA: "Cities, for Oliver, were not a part of nature. He could hardly feel, he could hardly admit even when it was pointed out to him, that cities are a second body for the human mind, a second organism, more rational, permanent and decorative than the animal organism of flesh and bone: a work of natural yet moral art, where the soul sets up her trophies of action and instruments of pleasure."*

———

CITIES IN THE WEST (the Bay Area, for instance). Despite the 7 million people, there was very little civilization to be had. What you had instead (hopefully, anyway, for at least a little while longer) was nature — nature in constant contention with the surrounding overcrowding and hurry. Only nature had ever come anywhere near a point of apotheosis. It was only nature, strangely enough, that could make you truly civilized.

---

* From Santayana's *The Last Puritan*

O NCE, WHEN LEAVING THE AIRPORT at midnight, I watched a coyote lope across the overpass in front of my car, headed toward the vast asphalt vacancy of a Target parking lot.

Fathering

S ITTING BESIDE MY FOUR-YEAR-OLD SON'S BED as he sleeps. One moment he seems to wake: his eyes open and he looks at me — and he's unsurprised, apparently, to find me there. Does he imagine that I am, or his mother is, always sitting there, every time he sleeps? If not one of us, then a sleep guardian? An angel? A ghost? He knows himself, I think, to be watched over. So the sight of me there is unremarkable. He rolls and soon he's snoring again.

To be always, for this boy, a presiding protector. He started year 2 of preschool last month.

Writing

T HAT WONDERFUL, DELUSIONAL MIDPOINT of a work-in-progress. All energies are rallied, all confidence in place — unassailable. You can't imagine stopping. You can't remember not being steeped in this project.

———

THE NARROWING DOWN, the scraping away to the basis, the quest through fewer and fewer options, the steady resolve to persist toward that last gratifying sense of inevitability, the need to remove all alternatives for the sake of purity, finality, and natural resolution, the need to know the thing has become the only thing it could ever wish to be, has had all its *allness* fulfilled and every part of its destiny realized. All this, and yet knowing forever the vast and innumerable alternate endings. This could describe life, but I'm describing the art-making process. How alike they are, art and living. How alive one is, consequently, when working well.

———

LEONARD BERNSTEIN: "Let me put it this way. Many, many composers have been able to write heavenly tunes and respectable fugues. Some composers can orchestrate the C-major scale so that it sounds like a masterpiece, or fool with notes so that a harmonic novelty is achieved. But this is all mere dust — nothing compared to the magic ingredient sought by them all: *the inexplicable ability to know what the next note has to be.*

Beethoven had this gift in a degree that leaves them all panting in the rear guard. When he really *did* it — as in the funeral march of the *Eroica* — he produced an entity that always seems to me to have been previously written in Heaven, and then merely dictated to him. We know with what agonies he paid for listening to the divine orders. But the reward is great. There is a special space carved out in the cosmos into which this movement just fits, predetermined and perfect. ... Form is only an empty word, a shell, without this gift of inevitability; a composer can write a string of perfectly molded sonata-allegro movements, with every rule obeyed, and still suffer from bad form. Beethoven broke all the rules, and turned out pieces of breathtaking rightness. Rightness — that's the word! When you get the feeling that whatever note succeeds the last is the only possible note that can rightly happen in that instant, in that context, then chances are you're listening to Beethoven."*

Corresp.

D EAR IHAB,   What you call my "amplitude" in one place is, I know it, tangled up with the "naiveté" you identify elsewhere. If I tend toward excess in my books — and something similar in correspondence, I think it

* From Bernstein's *The Joy of Music*

owes to my early decision to "go it alone," to live, learn, and work by instinct and consequently without guidance (beyond what books could afford me). If I can stand to better learn the language of restraint — and I do have much to learn in this area and others — I believe I'm destined to learn it slowly, or by the same method of gradual self-correction that has taught me whatever I now know about literature, the discourse concerning it, and the way its adherents talk to one another. For moments at a time I've considered how many obstacles I set myself, both aesthetically and materially, by taking so slow a road — not getting a conventional education, etc. One impairment is the innocence (or ignorance) revealed in my Guggenheim statement: I had not a clue that MFA Programs propounded W.C. Williams ("no ideas but in things"). In fact, I felt (humiliating as it is to admit) that I'd personally discovered in Williams's postulation a worthy ideal for fiction — one, ironically, that much MFA-brand writing would do well to espouse. This comes of my acquaintance with Williams man-to-man, entirely to the exclusion of things said *about* Williams. I might have been his first reader, which is wonderful for inspiration but horribly unhelpful as a credential — and I see how my Guggenheim statement can only have seemed to mouth a conventional wisdom. (An unfortunate — or anyway embarrassing — part of my slow maturation is that it should occur somewhat publicly.)

Library

As EARLY AS ALEXANDRIA in the third century B.C.,
a library was a secular temple embodying all the
inquisitive energy of a people aspiring to the status of
civilization. The definition of the word "civilize" itself is
an apt description of library purpose: "To bring out of a
barbarous stage of society. To enlighten, refine, and
educate." This Central Library alone, I realized as I
entered the second-floor Periodicals room, is an
"information economy" as quietly dynamic as the one on
the web — but different because more mysterious, and
more mysterious because more private. Of course,
libraries also encompass the web's riches: in Periodicals,
17 of some 20 Internet stations were in use. But what
touched me while wandering the enormous rooms was
the serene actuality of the collections. Library materials
amount to a vital cultural record available at no cost, no
strings attached, free of flashing ads or behavioral data
monitoring — except for a librarian's shush, maybe. A
patron was pulling books, tucking some under arm,
replacing others. What happens amid these aisles is
something sensorial, something personal because
essentially physical. I'll never "Google" every author,
scientific discovery, or school of thought contained in
the Central Library, but here, because they've been
arranged altogether at arm's length, I'll certainly
happen upon some. The library is meticulously
organized but breeds chance discoveries. It's public and

yet serene. You're never alone in the library but your privacy is safer than almost anywhere.

———

SHAKESPEARE: "Come, go with us, we'll guide thee to our house, and show thee the rich treasures we have got which, with ourselves, are all at thy dispose."

———

WITH FAMILIARITY TO A THING attention tends to slacken. But a writer's work often consists of remembering (or reminding) how it feels to be out of one's skin. It can be extremely valuable, even useful, to court strangeness. This is what I have in mind in my accounts of the library — to spend a while in the place as if for the first time.

———

STANDING AMID THE STACKS, I see anew how patchy all my understanding is. These innumerable eclectic, enlightening, amusing, eccentric, provocative, and frequently boring books remind me by their physical force of presence that knowledge is never a destination, always an aspiration. No single human memory can store all that is stored here in the collective memory of these books.

———

THE LIBRARY is dedicated to the worthy notion of civic *dignity*. (Adult literacy and citizenship classes, prison and shelter services, curated content amid a culture of chaotic fragmentation, analog quietude amid incessant media and nonstop technologically enabled gossip.)

This month begins my second year as a public scholar, facilitating discussions in Oregon communities about e-books and "the act of reading in the digital age."

Writing

TODAY, WAITING WITH ME in the lobby of the Thai restaurant as our to-go order was prepared, my son pointed out the blinking effect of the ceiling lights, created by the turning of a ceiling fan. "Daddy, let's imagine that the fan is juggling the lights!" My work — no matter all the study, all the re-writing, all the hours at the desk — ought to aspire toward this kind of freshness.

Fathering

WHEN YOU WERE BORN, I was the age you are now. I pray you've come through safely. (But does anyone?)

Since your first hour I've been praying, straining to save you from a fall by the power of mind alone. We never know, before, the way the heart wants to stretch open like a hand the size of the world. You were two days old and I, in an empty hospital ward, hallucinated your cry. Or did I really hear you from clear across the city? Later, despite myself, I would lose my grip and become my own worst idea of fatherhood. Maybe it will happen to you. We learn this way. We go easier on our dads. I kicked your toys and, turning, saw the disbelieving fear in your face. "I didn't mean to," I said. "They were underfoot." *Please believe me.* In that moment, you did. You saw I was telling the truth. Together we could uncomplicate anything.

Corresp.

DEAR IHAB,   I've often thought about the peculiar good my innocence has done me also. Without it I doubt I'd ever have completed or published a novel, let alone two — I mean given the long odds, the biases of the marketplace, and the tendency of these things to foster cynicism and inertness. And I can't help but wish that the Guggenheim auditors, if disconcerted by my naiveté, had traced it to its roots, which I believe are honorable artistically and which might have further pled my case (the "career narrative" I sent them ought to have helped here). On a related note, I've often wondered if *Lost Son** is not a bit of a special case where restraint is concerned, in that Rilke himself is so peculiar a figure, and in that his own dark lyrical naiveté — and his vulnerability born of inexperience — is necessarily such a part of *Lost Son*'s fabric, as is mine in the role of pilgrim (over-earnest probably) in those pages. Exuberance, unabashedness, unprotectedness, literary/intellectual innocence, bold lyricism: these are pigments I see in Rilke's ghost when it stands against the light. These *are* Rilke, and they inhered in the very experiment of *Lost Son*. Ultimately, late on, the experiment taught me that it is perhaps artistically impossible to evoke such qualities roundly, in a manner able to effect in readers an experience approximate to that of the innocent, unabashed Rilke. Such qualities are all potential aesthetic quagmires. (Here's one facet of the book about which many otherwise perceptive readers were mistaken: it does not try to emulate Rilke stylistically, and the stylistic oddities and exuberance throughout are also not an inadvertent overegging.

---

* *Lost Son*: my second published novel, inspired by the life and work of poet Rainer Maria Rilke, whom I'd been reading since I was 14. The book appeared when I was 29.

They are not signs of "purple" on the part of the author, but depictions of Rilke's own *overwhelm*, the heightened stimuli of his own *pre-poetic apprehensions* — that is, they seek to represent his unmediated sensorial experience prior to the transmutations of these that gave rise to his art.) I could not — or I did not wish to — write a book about Rilke ironically. The poet himself came as close as anyone, in *The Notebooks of Malte Laurids Brigge*, to accomplishing the artistically impossible as I've described it. And while writing, I often saw my novel as an homage to *Malte*, but of course my task in *Lost Son* was a far less natural product of its age. Rilke's book went purely forward. My novel retracts, retraces, and resurrects (or tries to).

———

"LET YOUR DEAFNESS no longer be a secret, even in art." —note by Beethoven on sketches for his Razumovsky Quartets, 1806

———

"IT MAY BE THAT WE ARE INTERESTED in any art only just so long as it is in process of search; that what moves us is the mysterious energy of quest."
   —Lionel Trilling, "Art and Fortune"

Screen

SATURDAY, OCTOBER 20. I lead a conversation in Vernonia, Oregon. Eleven or twelve people turn out to the small public library, assembling around a long table in one of the library's two rooms. Outside it is stormy and wet, the season's first chill in the air. Inside, the library volunteers brew coffee and set out store-bought cookies. My presentation unfolds in a studious, attentive atmosphere, with most participants eagerly jotting notes. The subsequent conversation is lively from the start. Two in the group say they own e-reading devices and use them regularly — but not to the exclusion of print books. All other participants clearly take issue with the increasingly digital format of most media. Since they are of retirement — or near-retirement — age, I find this to be something of a turnaround from prior programs (where the more avid adopters of e-reading have proven to be older folks). Of greatest interest to this Vernonia group are questions and controversy relating to reader privacy, problems of media consolidation, and the prospective corporate or government control of information. "In a sense," says a 60-something gentleman in one unforgettable moment, "digital text is harder to hold onto than print, and that's a problem. But another problem with digital is that it's harder to erase the stuff you might wish erased. Everything you do online leaves a trail, and that information will be on a server somewhere forever." He clutches a piece of paper to his chest. "This paper is mine. I know where it is, I can hold onto it and see what it says, I can throw it away. But who knows what that chimera of the screen will say about me. I can't erase that information even if I want to."

———

F ROM GARRET KEIZER'S PROFOUND LITTLE BOOK *Privacy* (p.88). "We would do well to ask if the capitalist economy and its obsessions with smart marketing and technological innovation cannot become as intrusive as any authoritarian state."

———

I T'S TAKEN FOR GRANTED that we are all, each of us, individual news & media processors. At what point does "information access" impede the ability to reflect meaningfully on what one reads, to form associations, to feed free thought and real creativity? *A picture is worth a thousand words.* And today's techno-boosterism would have us believe, vis-à-vis e-reading devices (that is, all devices), that a screen is worth a thousand books. An age of accelerated, hyper-disseminated simulacra, faux equivalencies, and deceptive approximations — and it's all patently there in the techno-lexicon: "e-book," "social profile," "augmented reality," &c. Have we really begun to mistake images of things for the things themselves?

Library

PASSING THROUGH THE LIBRARY STACKS again on my way out, I'm in a state of dreamy concentration. The library has altered me in the hours since my arrival. The high empty space above the books seems to hum with the din in a thousand other heads, the prior thoughts of strangers, students, writers — an immense cumulative labor of mind and spirit. I fall in with the stream of visitors heading downstairs. Being members of a democracy, we share many things. But what do we share more palpably than this space? Here in the public library, all is empirically ours. Tangible democratic resources await our daily use. The paper-scented air shares the rich mustiness of a garden. To breathe it in, surrounded by countless neatly labeled spines, is to prime the body for inspiration, that most useful byproduct of awe. The library has said to us: *look at all the fertile mind of man and woman has produced! What will your contribution be?*

———

Writing

F OR MY FELLOWSHIP APPLICATION to the Oregon
Arts Commission:

The following are some general tenets of my practice
at present. Of course I do not intend that they should
ever harden into doctrine (change and reinvention are
the prerogatives of any artist). • I take the primary
material of fiction to be individual human
consciousness. • I'm generally uninterested in the
massive, so-called "social" novel that is held to be the
ideal of any Great American work of fiction — work in
which the collective is of central importance. • I tend to
doubt the existence of any actual collective. Even a
social movement can only consist of individuals. • As
neuroscientist Giuli Tononi has recently said,
"Consciousness is synonymous with experience. Only
consciousness — singular — is really real." • I believe
that the world as we know it is constituted of
innumerable singulars, individual persons each unique
in his or her consciousness. • We are each only
ourselves — spheres, said Emerson, that may touch
other spheres. • Any sum societal total is never of
greater importance than the persons themselves. •
Today it's as vitally important as ever to emphasize
these things, given the widespread desire to upload and
exponentialize individual identity into a mass mind via
technology. (Aldous Huxley: "However hard they try,
men cannot create a social organism, they can only

create an organization. In the process of trying to create an organism they will merely create a totalitarian despotism."*) • Individual consciousness — the human capacity for idiosyncrasy — should be vitally affirmed. A plurality of literary styles, an ecosystem of artistic independence. • With peculiarly enduring power, fiction can represent individual consciousness. Every singularly constructed sentence can be a vessel for it, an honoring of it. From a single writer, great ranges of experience empathetically depicted. • It has always been the chief project and subject of literature to do this, to refer us beautifully outward to one another's discrete experience. • For these reasons the writer, whom the work of imagination renders honoree and outcast, is everywhere and nowhere at home, "continually in for and filling some other body" (said Keats). • The fiction writer augments through narrative's reach the possibility of understanding.

———

I'VE REACHED AN IMPASSE with my new novel, temporary I hope. Still, the longer I sit with them, the pages acquire secrets. A good thing. You work for this always. You want the pages to know more than you do. That way they can lead you. The struggle for control,

---

* From Huxley's *Brave New World Revisited*

the doubt about a thing's direction, the sense of manipulating the material — all that awkwardness goes away. You are free because the work is free. You can give yourself up to it. Your task is to let go, to listen. I'm on the brink of this. The important thing now is to wait — but to wait in the most active way possible. To remain in attendance. To keep myself available. "Being inactive with confidence," Rilke called this.*

————

"I HAVE HOURS OF UNSPEAKABLE REACTION against my smallness of production; my wretched habits of work — or of un-work; my levity, my vagueness of mind, my perpetual failure to focus my attention, to absorb myself, to look things in the face, to invent, to produce, in a word." —Henry James, journal, autumn 1882

Time

MY SON'S SENSE OF TIME: "Yesterday" is the time before his nap. When I tell him we will do something "later," i.e., after his nap, he asks: "Is 'later' today?"

————

* From Rilke's letter to Tora Holmstroem, 24 August 1904

T EILHARD DE CHARDIN: "Be pleased yet once again to come down and breathe a soul into the newly formed, fragile film of matter with which this day the world is to be freshly clothed."

———

T HE USE OF APOSTROPHES to abbreviate dates when we write them down: '02, '12, etc. This is a workaday means of admitting our own mortality. We're well aware of the unlikeliness of being mistaken for writing today's note in the year 2112.

———

O FTEN IN OLD PHOTOGRAPHS from artist colonies or literary conferences you'll see a caption something like: "Bottom row, left: unidentified man." What is it to become a mystery in an old photograph (or not even as much as a mystery)? Only this, maybe: to be dematerialized into the holy privacy of one's day-to-day labors. To let the indescribable, unshareable process swallow you up. What is fame, what is posterity, compared to the secret irrevocable glory of having had one's work?

———

"WE MAY BE IN A CRUCIAL BATTLE now between experience/meaning and some such thing as mere, indifferent duration." —David Thomson, *Television: A Biography*

Corresp.

DEAR IHAB,   So maybe *Lost Son* is necessarily a failure of sorts, engendering as it must the "fraughtness" your Australian friend pointed out in it. (This is not to deny its more ordinary failings.) But I'm glad to have made my attempt, and can't help but feel that the attempt itself has, in its very innocence, in its honest intention and naïve impossibility, a flawed beauty. You've been very kind to affirm this — to take the book seriously, in other words. I wonder what you would say with respect to these thoughts on "the impossible." I lived so long with *Lost Son*, as with Rilke — I've grown up *through them both* in so many ways, that I can't believe I delude myself or make excuses talking like this. Anyway, I console myself that I'm attempting something comfortably less than the impossible in my new novel. Then again, maybe a book is never wholly a possible thing. Whether or not *Lost Son* is a special case, your point about restraint is well taken. And I agree with John Dewey that "restraint, in art, is not identical with constraint." My cruder impulses are plain to see in much of my other published work. They stand out like ill-sized rivets, my naïf's hardware, for I've sought to construct worthy things using just the rough materials at hand. But I learn and learn (not a little from advice like yours), confident that these rivets will get pounded smooth. I remain grateful for your confidence — and generous encouragement too.

Writing

THOUGHT WHILE LISTENING to a performance of Beethoven's 1810 septet, with its virtuosic demands upon the violinist: why shouldn't a great book require as much skill of its reader, that the reader be expected to play all the "notes" in the book's composition? Quick, complex, expressive, adagio — all? The notes are more than the words. To play is more than simply to scan.

———

ALL THIS RELATES, I think, to the experience — more and more common for me as a reader — of being exhausted by novels that seem to get tied down to the prosaic processes of their own stories, the diagrammatic mechanisms of plot, of one scene following another, etc., novels which, in the end, are too much about their own subject, at the expense of also being (or even primarily being) about *expression*, sensibility, the lens of complex consciousness. Novels that have no need of me, no need of my co-creative sensibility as a reader. Novels that exist arbitrarily, inertly in their own transparent zone, indifferent to the chemistry of the reader's imaginative attention. I want a book to need me, to need the symbiosis of my readerly skill and my interpretive alertness.

———

J OSEPH BRODSKY, NOBEL SPEECH: "If what distinguishes us from other members of the animal kingdom is speech, then literature — and poetry in particular, being the highest form of locution — is, to put it bluntly, the goal of our species."

———

W HAT I MISS AS A READER is the audacious sensibility; the dimensionality of complex structure; the true idiosyncrasy of style (which is not the same as ventriloquism or mere eccentricity of voice). And it's not that I doubt that writing of this kind is being done. Only that I see the dictates of a marketplace bearing down, more and more, upon the creative impulse, and most noticeably upon decisions concerning what is to be published. A literature preoccupied with language and its potentialities, a work that presumes to consist of sentences, is a work presumed to have "little to say." We seem all too content, sometimes, to view work of this kind — work driven by the motive to *render* — as the mostly outmoded business of the pre-screen narrative, the old-fashioned literature of the last two centuries.

Screen

NOVEMBER 29TH, A RAINY EVENING in Sherwood, I lead a conversation for five or six avid, initially very shy attendees. One person, a woman in her fifties, states that she has a long background of working in Silicon Valley. While she's clearly appreciative of the benefits of interactive technologies generally and e-books specifically, she's strikingly quick to point out the undesirable prospects of a total switchover to electronic reading, expressing concern about the neurological implications of prolonged screen exposure. In attendance with her is her daughter, a seven-year-old who attends an online learning academy which requires all students to be logged on for a minimum of six hours daily. This young girl also makes a number of poignant comments about her preference for print books and her own dislike of intensive computer interaction. Near the program's close, a thirty-something woman, very quiet till this point, begins to speak with great eloquence of her regard for the special human properties of print books, including the experience afforded by second- or third-hand books of connecting the copy's current reader to readers past through markings on the pages, items left in the book, etc. "I appreciate e-reading devices," she says, "I use one now and then. But I feel so much more connected to other people — even to the author — when I'm reading a real book." To this an older gentleman responds with audible emotion — the evening's most memorable moment: "You know, I'm almost eighty now, and I've never heard a young person explain so precisely the way I also feel about books! That's just wonderful!"

———

TUESDAY, DECEMBER 4TH at Portland's Hollywood Library I lead a conversation with a dozen people. It's an eager, talkative group, and almost every person offers unique, deeply insightful observations. This from a twenty-something attendee taking meticulous notes (I paraphrase): "What occurs to me is that as the barriers to information access disappear, and as everything, including books, becomes available to any of us at any moment through our screens, we actually lose something in the bargain. We used to believe that interactive technologies would unite us, but actually they are splitting us into smaller and smaller communities." I, in response: "Marshall McLuhan referred to the way our technologies tend to shrink the world, creating what he called a 'global village.' But your feeling is that actually these tools are turning the world into a sprawling collection of micro-villages?" Answer: "Yes. We begin to believe we can absorb everything, but actually we are not really *committing* to anything."

———

ANOTHER REMARK, from a forty-something school librarian: "When the form of the book changes — or actually disappears — that's not all that changes. What changes, also, is our relationship to the words, to the author, and to one another as readers. Without a printed book in hand we start to feel less connected, and one consequence is that our responsibilities as readers feel less important. Our responsibilities to the author and to each other."

Time

DOWN IN FLORENCE, OREGON my grandmother passed away on December 6th. A largely painless death.

One of her last statements to my mother: "Love your neighbor."

Civics

IN LIGHT OF the horrendous gun killings here in Clackamas and in Sandy Hook, CT, the words of Joseph Brodsky keep coming to mind. "What concerns me is that man, unable to articulate, to express himself adequately, reverts to action. Since the vocabulary of action is limited, as it were, to his body, he is bound to act violently, extending his vocabulary with a weapon where there should have been an adjective."

———

IS IT ABSURD OR INAPPROPRIATE or disrespectful of this week's innocent dead to look at these killings as relating, in some not insignificant way, to the absence of a rich and aesthetically mature cultural life amongst most people in this country, an unfamiliarity with mindful creative expression? Is it somehow pathetic or outrageous, in such a moment, to consider the *civilizing* effects that a healthier arts system might have in the fabric of our fraying society? (This is not to suggest that the arts are, in themselves, a panacea against societal breakdown, a suggestion already contradicted by the end of Germany's Weimar Republic and events in early 20th-century Vienna.)

———

Václav Havel, "Politics and Conscience." "We must trust the voice of our conscience more than that of all abstract speculations and not invent other responsibilities than the one to which the voice calls us. We must not be ashamed that we are capable of love, friendship, solidarity, sympathy and tolerance, but just the opposite: we must set these fundamental dimensions of our humanity free from their 'private' exile and accept them as the only genuine starting point of meaningful human community. We must be guided by our own reason and serve the truth under all circumstances as our own essential experience. [...] It surely makes much more sense to operate in the sphere of causes than simply to respond to their effects. By then, as a rule, the only possible response is by equally immoral means. To follow that path means to continue spreading the evil of irresponsibility in the world."

Time

Last night, after midnight, I awoke to a soft sustained scraping along the back of the house, the storm windows rattling. Our apricot tree is down. The bare canopy, horizontal now, fills the yard. Its soil soaked, its roots rotted, it lay itself down, slowly, in a kind of resignation, and didn't so much as scrape the paint from our house's cedar shakes.

———

T UESDAY, JANUARY 1ST. Our son tells my wife before bed that he intends to dream he is the captain of a boat, the toy boat from *The Cat in the Hat*. And takes a toy replica to bed with him for the purpose. Morning of January 2nd he confirms his success: "I dreamt I was a sea captain. I was sailing the toy boat. I sailed from Portland to Santa Cruz!"

———

J ANUARY 2ND. My wife and I each commenting, at random and repeatedly these last few days, on how much we love our little house. We've been away in California for a week and a half. This love of home owes to our absence but is no less real for that. It's simply a matter of the valuable act of returning. The greater the number of occasions we're given to come back to this house from a journey, the more profoundly our ownership — our grateful stewardship — becomes felt.

I've resolved, beginning this year, to take better care of it. It is little, it's imperfect, but for now it is ours.

——

T ODAY WE TAKE DOWN the Christmas lights. The tree is hauled away for recycling. The ornaments are back in their boxes. The cold clings to one's jacket after coming indoors, demanding the jacket be sluffed right away, despite one's chill.

——

T HOSE ANTIQUE PHOTOS of people, families, babies, husbands and wives, ancestral homes, which the antique sellers sell out of old cigar boxes for a quarter each. What scattered lives and abandoned memories do these represent? How many dead and gone, dearly departed, can the world's nooks and crannies accommodate? How much of this free-floating memory does narrative — commodious, generous narrative — catch?

——

(I'VE BEEN AWARDED an individual artist fellowship from the Oregon Arts Commission. I write them a stirring note of thanks.)

Screen

JANUARY 20TH. I lead a conversation at a community center in Alpine (Monroe). 22 people turn out, gathering amiably in the chilly, somewhat cavernous ex-church, a long cinderblock structure recently acquired and converted for community use. The atmosphere is warm, inclusive, intelligent. The cold, fog, and frost rub at the windows, but we get down to business. At one point the discussion turns to the massive storage capacity of electronic reading devices, and somebody raises the insightful question: "How many books can a person *actually read* at one time?" There's a feeling in this group that when measuring the value of one's reading experience, quantity is not necessarily an automatic enhancement. Instead, sustained focus, meaningful immersion, etc., seem more highly prized. This spurs a substantive dialogue about "needs and desires" being "implanted" in consumers by product manufacturers, advertisers, etc.

———

THE MORE THE BOOK AS WE KNEW IT got drawn into the realm of social media, the more we started expecting it to "perform" in accordance with social media norms and standards.

"T HE FUTURE isn't what it used to be."
—Paul Valery

———

S TILL, ALWAYS, EVEN IN THE QUIET of your room you face the onslaught. Endlessly you work to clear your vision against the day's overcrowding. You seek a single coherent narrative of thought, the prolonged extension of a tone amid the broken broadcast noises, antic and ever-changing. You school yourself in history. You labor to remember: underlying the current complexity is woeful oversimplification. Meanwhile you will know the truth by the serene simplicity of its surface. A shimmer, beneath which: depth, profundity, the unbroken quietude of the real.

Writing

D OESN'T THE SHEET grow infinitesimally heavier with each word written upon it? Doesn't each thought acquire greater substance and mass through the process of writing, its embodiment in ink? There *is* weight to this work. It is not all abstraction and philosophy — or,

what would be worse, pure cogitation. No. What makes
the work real is that it can be added to a scale, hung in
actual balance. Working, reading, you seek an authentic
tug, as a hand that holds an object is pulled toward the
ground. We want gravity — a footing in ourselves, or,
one at a time, in each other.

———

The vault and scope of schooling
And mastery in the mind,
In silk-ash kept from cooling,
And ripest under rind —
What life half lift the latch of,
What hell stalks towards the snatch of,
Your offering, with dispatch, of!
　　　　—G.M. Hopkins

Time

DAILYNESS: THE SOOTHING BEAUTY OF IT,
sometimes. Sometimes it seems full of reassurance, of
affirmation, of benediction, like a picture by Chardin.
The puddles in the pavement along our street, where
the potholes and rough surfaces are. Some days they've
meant dejection. Today they seemed worthy of a
passing admiration, so humbly picturesque, familiar,
comely.

F EBRUARY 2ND. While driving from Prineville through the iced-over forests on the slopes of Mount Hood, headed through the 4 A.M. darkness to the Portland airport (to fly to California for my grandmother's forestalled memorial service), I tell my wife about my weird dream of the night before. I'd borrowed the car of novelist William Gay (a man I met once, and who died recently). I'd taken Gay's car on a long, long drive. It was a large, powerful car with a very smooth ride. But getting out at my first stop I found the driver's side front tire in tatters, the wheel itself horribly misshapen. The three other tires, also, were fragmenting, bound to fall apart any minute. The rest of the dream revolved around my anxiety over this. How to get where I was going? How to explain the car's condition when I brought it back to William? I say to my wife, "Obviously that was all about my anxiety anticipating this drive." Several minutes pass, the road hissing unnervingly beneath us, sheeted in ice, heavily fogged over in places. Then my wife says, "Are you sure the dream wasn't about your life as a writer?" A vehicle borrowed, she points out, from a novelist I hugely admired, a novelist who is no longer with us. A big powerful vehicle, and yet it has its own mysterious problems. You can't be sure just how far you'll get, how well it will hold up on such a long journey. She's correct, of course. And how it amazes me that I'd seen none of these obvious elements in the dream. Two days later, browsing a tiny selection of books at a thrift store in Santa Cruz, I find a first edition of William's story collection *I Hate to See That Evening Sun Go Down.*

———

WERE YOU A MOTHER? Did you stand nights at a sleeping child's door, listening for breath beyond the gurgling of rain in gutters and spouts? Were you a woodcarver? A bird keeper? Librarian? Were you clubfooted or a lover of dance? Did you read the leaves in the cup of every guest? Did you write and send letters and wait for letters back? Did you tell yourself a story all your days? Were you a swimmer, a gardener, a civil servant? Did you read books in the evening, in a chair beside the window? Did you walk daily to church, see the doctor but once every few years, put on hip boots and fish from the shallows? Did you teach school? Punch tickets? Were you a healer? A hunchback? A lover of music? Were you born where you lived? Did you marry? Could you remember earthquakes, storms, droughts, epidemics? Did you ever count out coins and ration food? Could you remember days of abundance? Did you love dogs? Did you watch morning's arrival over bodies of water? Did you share a bed, a daily meal, a drinking glass? Did you harbor jealousies? Were you

an architect, a glazier, a potter, a prostitute? Did you
know the loneliness of cities? Did you fling your hat
over borders? Did you cultivate memories? Were you a
neighbor? A baker? Did friends sit to drink coffee at
your table? Did you write and send letters? Did you
observe the holy days? Did you anoint your brow with
ash? Did you consider all the other gods? Were you
more often settled or moving? Did you celebrate? Did
you despair? Did you write and send letters?   (for the
new novel)

CITY SUITE:
i. Vienna Variations
ii. Dublin Variations
iii. Andalucía Variations
iv. Salzburg Variations

It is while traveling, while consenting to become a guest, that one awakens most vividly to — and confronts most enliveningly — one's persistent condition as guest in everyday life.

Stefan Zweig

i. Dreamers & Demagogues (Vienna Variations, 2015)

Instructions for the dreamer:

1) Wake up.
2) Try not to move.
3) Speak the last image you remember.
4) Take up your pen.*

HerenGracht

FRIDAY.   En route to Vienna I have the whole day in Amsterdam, so I visit the Rijksmuseum and wander the city. While crossing a canal I come upon a police scene, spectators crowding the bridge. On the water below, a tourist boat waits while a dredger's giant claw searches the depths. From an adjacent boat, a cameraman films the whole thing.

What are they looking for? A body? Bodies? The search seems a perfunctory process, but unsettling: every time the mechanical claw surfaces from the darkness below I brace myself for the sight of something grisly clutched amid rocks and slime.

---

* Dr. Micah Sadigh, "The Vienna Lectures" (2015)

I watch a long time, but finally move on, half disappointed, half relieved. Throughout the day, amid Amsterdam's narrow, colorful, photogenic houses and leafy cobblestone lanes, I find myself thinking constantly of Anne Frank and her family in their annex behind blackout curtains. Of their betrayal. Of the girl's diary splayed open on the floor after the Nazi raid. Every scenic bridge causes me to stop and spin on my heels snapping pictures, but all the while my mind is like that claw dredging the darkness.

Herz / Heart

SATURDAY. VIENNA. BELVEDERE GARDENS. This is my second visit to this city and again I wonder: what makes Vienna so elusive, so cloaked and chimerical, seemingly intangible despite its preponderantly dense and massive structures? One can know the landmarks, the historical chapters, names and dates, principal works of art, varieties of coffee and cake, even (to a degree) the language. Read your Freud, hear your Beethoven, smile at the many eccentricities of the Habsburg dynasty, stand aghast at the horrific paroxysms of the Second World War — still you are held at bay. The heart of Vienna remains closed to you. Instead the city envelops you in its elaborate artifice: Jugendstil sex and goldleaf, crown jewels, copper domes, horse-drawn carriages, and lemon-garnished schnitzel.

This valedictory city, vaporous and stable, dreamy and empirical. Sprinklers sweep the lawns of the Maria-Theresien-Platz, whispering *ringstrasse ringstrasse ringstrasse.*

———

Ich shaue nur.   I'm just browsing.

Wo ist Zweig?

In March 1938, the whole of [Vienna's] Hotel Imperial, from the café to the uppermost suite, was requisitioned by Nazi authorities for the reception of Hitler. ... And the Imperial remained the domain of Nazi officials throughout the war. Today the chairs, booth backs, and carpets of the Café Imperial are midnight blue and pale gold shades. When I went there in the middle of a Saturday afternoon, there were almost no customers. ... Waiters whisked in and out, zipping from one deserted room to the next. When I asked about the café's history in the 1930s and 40s, waiter after waiter shrugged and made a face as though I'd asked where the bathroom was in too loud a voice.
  —George Prochnik, *The Impossible Exile: Stefan Zweig at the End of the World*

*Bitte konnen Sie mir der weg nach Holocaust-Mahnmal
erklären?* Can you please tell me the way to the
Holocaust Memorial?

———

HOW CAN ONE AVOID COMPARING the state-sponsored memorials in present day Berlin to the near absence of these things in Vienna? Compare Berlin's open-air Topography of Terror exhibit or its massive Memorial to the Murdered Jews of Europe — which, so as to be unavoidable, is situated in the city center — to Vienna's much smaller, poorly marked Holocaust Memorial in the Judenplatz, or the bronze excrescence of that ugly Jewish caricature in the Albertinaplatz.* Consider the fact that until only recently, as noted by author George Prochnik, the permanent chronological exhibition in the Museum of the City of Vienna ended — halted abruptly — at World War I. Consider the prominently situated Ringstrasse statue of Karl Lueger, antisemitic establishment figure who in 1890, some years before becoming mayor of

---

* In 2021 Vienna unveiled its Holocaust Wall of Names, situated on a small square behind the enormous Votivkirche. Requiring twenty years of planning and negotiations before its opening, it occasions one to ask again, why so little so late?

Vienna, made the suggestion that Viennese Jews be herded onto a ship and sunk at sea. Consider the Austrian State Library's brand new, stylishly designed Literature Museum, which merely documents — but never so much as hints at the culpability of — those among the Viennese literati who collaborated with the Nazis, the so-called "occupiers."

Consider the Literature Museum librarian who, when I ask why the museum included only a single glancing reference to Stefan Zweig, flattened his mouth and explained that Zweig is not very well known in Austria, and seemed bemused by my inordinate interest in this ostensibly "minor" figure of Austrian letters. Jewish-born Zweig, child of Vienna, who was once among the most famous writers in Austria — and throughout Europe — and devoutly espoused himself to internationalism and made it his lifelong mission to be a multilingual citizen of the world, a passionate believer in the human community that transcends the political and dogmatic, who swore to himself "never to write a single word that affirmed war or disparaged another nation." Zweig, who while writing his memoir *The World of Yesterday* from exile in 1941 mournfully admitted his heartbreak at seeing his work totally effaced by the Nazis:

> Of the hundreds of thousands and even
> millions of my books which had their secure
> place in the book shops and in innumerable

homes in Germany, not a single one is obtainable today. ... Everything, or almost everything that represents my work in the world during forty years has been destroyed by one and the same fist. ... I could not adequately describe the fall into the abyss which I with countless others equally innocent suffered, if I did not indicate the height from which it occurred, and the singularity and consequences of this destruction of our whole literary generation, an occurrence unique in history.

Ein Traum Gescheitert / A Failed Dream

AS ONE WHO'S COME TO VIENNA to write, naturally I can't help asking: Doesn't Zweig deserve some reparations? If nothing else, this literary world-soul would make an ideal artistic symbol for a Vienna intent upon atonement. Is his present-day obscurity one indicator of the lack of will for such a thing? (While in the city, I do not ask these questions aloud.)*

---

* But returning to Vienna in 2022, I find the selfsame Literature Museum mounting a large exhibition dedicated to Stefan Zweig and his work. Entitled *Stefan Zweig: World Author*, it occupies a whole floor of the building, is advertised robustly via posters plastered all over Vienna, and runs for three months. What a difference seven years — or *eighty* — make.

"A nightmare is a failed dream," says Freud, words that could, perhaps, serve as a metaphorical statement about the tragedy and savagery of World War II Vienna, Freud's own city — and Zweig's city, where for much of its history as Zweig described it, a dream of unity seemed possible: "All the streams of European culture converged…and subconsciously every citizen became supernational, cosmopolitan, a citizen of the world." How nightmarish the city became after the Anschluss, the Nazi annexation.

Has the nightmare yet been adequately acknowledged? It seems to me that anyone possessing a conscience must ponder this question while walking about this city. Has Vienna transferred the black matter of the nightmare from the second mind of sleep to the waking one?

Where, for the writer, the artist, do these questions lead? Where, particularly when, at home, the demagoguery of the era so resembles that of the nightmare in question — fists pounded at podiums, the mocking of the marginalized, the extolling of deportations and border closures as public virtues, the incitements to thuggery and political hysterics.

Where do these questions lead when, here in present-day Europe, the stability of the European Union looks to be less than sound?

———

In Full Sun

"MY FATHER FOUGHT IN HITLER'S ARMY," my Viennese friend G. told me. This was 2012, on my first visit to Vienna. I had come with my family on a home exchange, and G., the sixty-something mother of the woman whose apartment we were borrowing, had appointed herself our tour guide. One afternoon she led us on a walk through the Innere Stadt, the old town, across the baroque courtyards of the Hofburg palace complex, and out to the broad open concrete and lawns of the Heldenplatz, where we stood in full summer sun. "I'm telling you this because it is important not to hide from it," G. said. "Too many are still hiding from what happened then. There were 200,000 people in this square on the day that Hitler gave his speech here — they were cheering at the top of their lungs, overjoyed. And today you can find hardly anyone who will admit to being there, or who will say, 'Yes, my parents were there,' or, 'My grandparents were there.' It is shameful."

Here and there around Vienna you see little bronze squares laid into the pavement before the doorways. Stolpersteine, they're called. Stumbling stones. You can find these in cities throughout Europe. Easily mistaken for electrical or plumbing outlets, they yield up, upon closer inspection, the names of people who were torn from their houses and deported to the Nazi camps. Some 65,000 Austrians met that fate.

If in Berlin they say, "We did this," in Vienna they seem to say, "The war is something that happened here." Surveys show that most Austrians continue to deny that 200,000 people welcomed Hitler's troops as they marched into Austria, despite the overwhelming evidence that ecstatic crowds gathered at Heldenplatz in Vienna's city center to hear him deliver a rousing speech.

———

The view most commonly held still is that the Anschluss was forced on a reluctant people.
— *The Telegraph*, UK, April 12, 2006

———

"Zweig is not considered very important here today," said the librarian.

———

Tut mir leid, aber ich bin ein Auslander.   I'm sorry, but I'm a foreigner.

———

The Ages

You are every age in your dreams. —Micah Sadigh, "Dreams and Creativity"

(Can one also, in one's dreams and waking reveries, find oneself *living* in every age?)

WEDNESDAY. The heat has finally broken in Vienna, yielding to rain much like it did during my time here three years back. I am out in the wet, walking, my shirt and cap soaked. I've decided to pay a visit to one of Beethoven's apartments.

Across the boulevard from the present-day university, three or four stark rooms are open to visitors. They are high up on the fourth floor of a building which is itself about four stories above street level, having been built on a remnant of the old city fortifications. In the first room you find a gorgeous blonde-wood, five-pedaled piano from the composer's day. Beyond it, on a pedestal between two windows, is Ludwig's stern bust in bronze.

I move slowly through the rooms, but find myself continually drawn back to the view from the windows in each. In the composer's time here (1804–1808), ramparts still stood where the Ringstrasse is today, and beyond his window he had a view of green. Nowadays the late 19th-century university building dominates the scene, and beyond that you see the twin spires of the massive

Votivkirche, the Votive Church, in their neo-gothic filigree.

Out of the front windows, much closer than both of these sights, is a contemporary office building, seven or eight stories, all glass and steel. Looking at that building, you look straight into a large conference room where, today, alone at the long wooden table amid seventeen empty chairs, a man in a white shirt sits with hands raised to the back of his head, elbows out, staring straight into Beethoven's apartment. We see each other, share an impulse to wave, then both pretend we are looking elsewhere.

While living here just over two hundred years ago, Beethoven worked on his fourth, fifth, seventh, and eighth symphonies, a few of the Razumovsky string quartets, and his opera "Fidelio." In two of the rooms are small stations where visitors can sit and listen through earphones to any of these pieces. Seated at one station, you look directly out the window into the windows of an 18th or 19th-century building across the way (on the Shreyvogelgasse). In those windows, too, you can see the goings-on of a modern office, or series of offices.

With the impassioned allegro molto of the Razumovsky Quartets in my headphones, I watch a woman in profile at her desk, speaking into a telephone headset. In another window one floor above her, a man sits at his computer monitor, motionless.

Was Beethoven's time more propitious than ours, more compensatory for a dreamer who would sit listening to the sounds in his mind? No. Outside these windows, in those days too, the world went on as it will, mostly indifferent.

A few minutes later, at the neighboring station, I listen to a glorious quartet of voices accompanied by a

slow set of orchestral bass tones from a section of
"Fidelio" called "Mir ist so wunderbar."

To be in these rooms with this music in your ears is
to sit for at least a few moments in Beethoven's mind
and body. But my thoughts remain on those people
across the street.

I hardly know what to make of these juxtapositions of
time and work. The long-dead composer somehow
survives in these empty rooms (if only by virtue of the
many visitors who come here seeking him). His music
seems to grow more and more miraculous — and more
relevant. Meanwhile, in our contemporary future twenty
feet from here, the inexpressive workaday world ticks
slowly onward for the honest employees at their desks.
And sometimes, in moments of boredom or idleness,
they turn — don't they? — and look across, straight
into these windows, straight at the composer's ghost.

Spool

WHETHER WE LIVE IN BEETHOVEN'S TIME or
our own, we cannot always choose what
we give our attention to. Time and
circumstance claim us to a degree, if not totally. And yet
our time and other times also coexist continually, and in
some mysterious moments we can see, vividly, their
crossing over. This gives us pause. We stop and look.
We may have thought our era stood alone in time, but

now we see the spool of the future tugging steadily at our threadlike days, as it tugged at theirs.

"Art is visionary," writes Jeanette Winterson. "It sees beyond the view from the window, even though the window is its frame. ... Art is not documentary. It may incidentally serve that function in its own way but its true effort is to open to us dimensions of the spirit and of the self that normally lie smothered under the weight of living."*

Ring Road

Kann ich etwas zu mitnehmen bestellen?   Can I order something to go?

WALKING VIENNA'S RINGSTRASSE is a strange experience. You encounter pure monumentalism and grandeur on display — and it's that verb, *display*, and not the marbled and crenellated nouns it refers to that draws your attention. The neo-gothic City Hall, the neo-classical Parliament building, the neo-Renaissance museums of the Maria-Theresien-Platz — they merely *display*. You want to bask in the beauty of those surfaces, you want to think, "Here's another Paris," but the overriding falsity frustrates your admiration. It's a state-sponsored

---

* From Winterson's *Art Objects*.

grotesquerie of set pieces, bygone times rebuilt in the 1880s. Fake from their beginnings, they were then re-faked following the devastation of World War II, and that re-faking is itself a complication deeply characteristic of this valedictory capital, this ambivalent, denial-prone "nervous splendor" of a city (as author Frederic Morton called it).

But also commingled in the Ringstrasse, however, is a fanciful yearning for the best that all the European epochs produced, those times before passports. And in that there *is* something beautiful: you do see — don't you? — a glimmer of Zweig's idealized City of the World. In his mesmerizing compendium *Cultural Amnesia*, Clive James captures something of Zweig's Viennese *Welt von Gestern*, and the contradictions this city's history so painfully exemplifies:

> In the late nineteenth and early twentieth centuries, Vienna was the best evidence that the most accommodating and fruitful ground for the life of the mind can be something more broad than a university campus. [...] Reading about old Vienna now, you are taken back to a time that should come again: a time when education was a lifelong process. You didn't complete your education and then start your career. Your education *was* your career, and it was never completed. For generations of writers, artists, musicians, journalists, and

mind-workers of every type, The Vienna café was a way of life. [...] Most, though not all, of the café population was Jewish, which explains why the great age of the café as an informal campus abruptly terminated in March 1938, when the Anschluss wrote the finish — *finis Austriae*, as Freud put it — to an era. It also explains why the great age had come to fruition in the first place. [...] The fate of the Jews [...] there could be no clearer proof that the mind is hard to kill. Nor could there be a more frightening demonstration of the virulent power of the forces which can combine to kill it.

The best and the worst of human behavior, human striving — Vienna gives example of it all. We are not alone in time, because all times are with us.

Strive

I T WAS FROM ONE OF THOSE BUILDINGS along the Ringstrasse, the Vienna Academy of Fine Arts, that a young Adolf Hitler descended the steps in 1908, embittered. For the second time he'd failed to gain admission as a student. Two years later Hitler wrote to a friend, "Do you know — without any arrogance — I still believe that the world lost a great deal by my not being able to go to the academy and learn the craft of painting."

The world lost a great deal.

The Vienna-born psychologist Alfred Adler believed that there are both negative and positive ways of striving for superiority (i.e., excellence, accomplishment). The desire for power and dominance motivate negative striving, while positive striving is motivated by a desire to inspire others and to improve the self. "Healthy people," Adler said, "strive to improve the culture."

Hitler the painter was a poseur and a hack, and his heart was already full of hate. So here's a dream: the young painter descends the steps, rejected, and then sticks madly to his brushes in some squalid quarter, painting scene after kitschy scene, obsessively deluded by his own work and resigned to obscurity as the artist's only sure allotment. And he's never heard from again.

What might the world *not* have lost then?

Humus

BACK AT HOME, amid the latest revolting pronouncements broadcast from the circuit of hateful campaign politics, my mind goes on dredging the darkness. I find myself rereading Václav Havel, Czech playwright, subversive, and statesman.

To Havel I bring the question: Where, in the midst of

incessant demagoguery, does the work of the artistic dreamer belong? What purpose can such dreaming serve?

In his famous 1978 essay "The Power of the Powerless," Havel speaks of "the political significance of those 'pre-political' events and processes that provide the living humus from which genuine political change usually springs." He goes on:

> The question of whether one or several political parties are in power, and how these parties define and label themselves, is of far less importance than the question of whether or not it is possible to live like a human being. [...] A genuine, profound, and lasting change for the better [...] will have to derive from human existence, from the fundamental reconstitution of people in the world, their relationships to themselves and to each other, and to the universe. [...] This is not something that can be designed and introduced like a new car. A better system will not automatically ensure a better life. In fact the opposite is true: only by creating a better life can a better system be developed.

An artist himself, Havel identified the arts among the vitally 'pre-political' — the arts as an attribute of, and an agent for, a better life. The arts as a living humus.

Even when art is not explicitly political in substance,

it remains politically relevant and vital. In a 1984 essay, "Six Asides about Culture," Havel asks whether any "meaningful cultural act" can ever be thought of as separate from "the common good."

> Is one not an integral part of the other from the start? Does not the bare fact that a work of art has meant something to someone — even if only for a moment, perhaps to a single person — already somehow changed, however minutely, the overall condition for the better? Is it not itself an inseparable component of that condition, transforming it by its very nature? And does not a change in conditions mediated by a cultural achievement open the door to further cultural achievements? Is not culture itself something that is a common good? Is not some 'improvement in conditions' — in the most general, the deepest, and, I would say, the existential sense of the word — precisely what makes culture culture? … Can we separate the awakening human soul from what it always, already is — an awakening human community?

———

Wake up. Try not to move. Speak the last image you remember. Take up your pen.

———

As AN ARTIST, AND INDEED LATER as a statesman who brought his artistic gifts to bear on his role, Havel knew what artistic thinking is about — that it's about the practice of re-envisioning oneself and one's world. It's about taking the long view while tending to the necessary (frequently mundane) intricacies of process. It's about inspiration and excellence, memory and enterprise, invention, entrepreneurship, lineage and legacy and belief. Artistic thinking is never less than thoroughly optimistic.

At its essence, art (like dreaming) consists of questions and conduces to enrichment and expansion via *uncertainty*. It's about being at ease with uncertainty to the extent of accommodating unconventional solutions. This is in contrast to propaganda, which concerns itself solely with "answers," a pugnacious surety obtained via incessant repetition (sometimes dogmatic but more often, nowadays, enticingly disguised).

Artistic imagination is the propensity to escape the confines of the self and the pressure of the self's narrow needs. It's the empathic ability to see and feel what "others" see and feel, the power to *express* all these things. As Zadie Smith explored eloquently in her 2008 lecture "Speaking in Tongues," art and artistic imagination require equivocation, the shape-shifting capacity. This honorable equivocation is endemic to the arts, and it is a kind of civic virtue. What we want is not an increasingly politicized art, but a *more artistic politics*.

Art is visionary. Art is not documentary.

What we want is a politics spun from the fiber of a polity, a society, a demos, in which the higher order of the arts and artistic thinking are integral, not extraneous — characteristic, not inconceivable.

"We will not know our own injustice if we cannot *imagine* justice," writes Ursula K. Le Guin in an essay entitled "A War without End." "We will not be free if we do not *imagine* freedom. We cannot demand that anyone try to attain justice and freedom who has not had a chance to *imagine* them as attainable." (Emphasis mine.)

Never forgetting what came before, whether in order to draw strength or outrage from it, the artistic thinker, the dreamer, moves forever forward, and the further he or she goes, the more deeply integrated he or she becomes in the human community.

Only by creating a better life can a better system be developed.

Instructions for the dreamer:

KEEP TRAVELING, KEEP LOOKING. Think again about windows, all the windows in this world, their views, those rooms, all the hours inside them, all the darkness and sins of the history once held in these rooms and watched from these windows, and all the human imaginativeness and wonder too.

Consider the work you are doing and the days that are passing.

Look at what claims you and ask, Is it good? Meaning: Will it give some kind of goodness to others?

Sit down to your desk and say to the sounds in your mind, I'm listening.

ii. Abandoned City (Dublin Variations, 2016)

The Uncreated Conscience

THE FERRY WAS MASSIVE: twelve decks high, four onboard restaurants, a kids' arcade and fun house, designated family play areas, a two-screen cinema, a casino, one club class lounge, one public, nearly three miles of auto parking space, an extensive duty-free shop replete with parfumerie and jewelry cases, and, way up on Deck 11, a sea-air promenade with views in all directions and specified smoking shelters. The ferry was called THE ULYSSES. Beside the gleaming onboard reception desk hung an enormous portrait of James Joyce, carved in relief from a great panel of unvarnished wood. For onboard dining, you had your choice of Leopold Bloom's Traditional Irish Pub, Boylan's Brasserie, or Café Lafeyette. Deck 10's semicircular lounge with plush recliners was christened after the author, and at key spots throughout Deck 9 along the Ulysses Walking Tour were posted informational displays about Joyce's magnum opus.

The nearly 2,000 passengers, as far as one could tell, were not terribly interested in the ferry's literary namesake or the novel's author. Despite the prevalent invocations of Joyce and his work, nobody was overheard taking up the Joycean theme, not a soul was observed to stop and read the walking tour displays, and as I stood up top in the sun and ferocious wind of the promenade with Holyhead's green coastline diminishing in the wake and Ireland an emerald sliver on the horizon ahead, I couldn't help thinking of the final page of *A Portrait of the Artist as a Young Man* — Stephen Dedalus bidding farewell, much as Joyce himself did in 1904, to his homeland:

> Mother is putting my new secondhand
> clothes in order. She prays now, she says, that
> I may learn in my own life and away from
> home and friends what the heart is and what
> it feels. Amen. So be it. Welcome, O life! I go
> to encounter for the millionth time the reality
> of experience and to forge in the smithy of my
> soul the uncreated conscience of my race. ...
> Old father, old artificer, stand me now and
> ever in good stead.

The irony — the irony I couldn't ignore, both here aboard this gargantuan boat named in homage to his book, and later while walking the streets of the city that so actively claims him (and claims to honor him) — is that James Joyce, like so many other artists and writers of note in his time and after, left Ireland permanently. In his case, he quit the place in earliest adulthood, never returning save for a few brief visits.

Joyce left because in Dublin almost all he saw was "paralysis," the paralysis he would portray in multiple permutations throughout the stories in *Dubliners*. But as I reflect on my own visits to Dublin — my first alone in the bitter fall of 1997, and my second during this summer of nearly twenty years later — it's not the paralysis theme so much as that phrase from Dedalus, "the uncreated conscience of my race," that lingers so troublingly in my mind. Through his doppelganger Joyce claimed, with that sentence, a personal responsibility. He would bring to realization within himself something that, as he saw it, those around him in the culture and society of Dublin never had — and he feared perhaps never would. He would realize an *identity*.

November Town

"The history of Dublin is its failure to match the industrialization of England."
—Dr. Conor McNamara, Dublin bus tour, July 4, 2016

IN THE FRIGID, WET NOVEMBER OF 1997 I spent three days walking the empty streets of Dublin. I'd come from two months spent in London and by comparison Dublin struck me as sleepy, understated, drab, and sad. Everywhere I went I seemed to sense a kind of weariness, a feeling of general (perhaps generational) fatigue. The city seemed an eerie, haunting, leftover kind of place, gritty and decrepit in many quarters, and it had a raw tinge of urban danger after dark. It felt nothing like a "destination." More, it seemed — and how to put this? — it seemed to suffer a lack of distinctive identity, to be a place abandoned and disowned in many deep indescribable ways.

The pains and tensions of Ireland's "troubles" were still alive in that time. Bill Clinton was at work behind the scenes helping to facilitate a peace agreement involving the IRA. The euro's day had not yet come. The consolations and revivifications of the new globalized Europe would reach this far northwestern outpost only slowly. But finally, in the course of the next decade, changes did come to Dublin, or so I heard whenever I compared notes with friends and family who visited in those years. There had been an economic boom (the so-called Celtic Tiger), the euro had been adopted, there was gentrification, jobs aplenty. All this had, reportedly, injected a new vitality into the place (along with the complications that arise with wealth). So on my return this July, even while expecting to see evidence of the 2008 global economic collapse, I was prepared to find a newly vibrant capital. Instead, it surprised me to receive strongly, again, those same impressions from my visit of two decades prior. Whether walking along the Liffey or navigating the spidery channels of Dublin's oldest streets, I found that the feeling of "new" Dublin was different in ways only superficial: crowds on the sidewalks, more coffee shops, more blandly ubiquitous global entities like Starbucks, Subway, and the Apple Store, and a fancified Grafton Street complete with all the predictable brands in all the predictably glittering window displays.

Meanwhile, unlike other bustling European capitals large and small, there was the persistent peculiar air of aimlessness about this city — ironic, surely, given the ferocity of the battles here from 1916 on. Even amid the summertime noise of tourists and rowdy pub-goers and amplified buskers, Dublin seemed to remain, at its more secret core, a subdued and faintly barren place, a city like a creature resigned to having one leg in a trap. I don't quite know how else to articulate the weird specificity of this effect that Dublin has on me. It's a hard thing to put your finger on, but when you're there the city digs out a hollow in your chest.

Rather than abating, has this hollowness — this nowhere-in-particularness of Dublin — been exacerbated by the arrival of globalism? Probably in a city as long-abused, as embattled, and ultimately disowned as Dublin, a global economic boom can forge at most only an ersatz "newness." Meanwhile, globalism's material benefits are hardly universal. The 10% corporate tax-rate may delight and reward the likes of Intel and Pfizer and Starbucks, but, as historian Conor McNamara pointed out during a city bus tour, there are currently 29,000 units of state housing in the neighborhood of Dublin's Guinness Brewery (its largest tourist attraction), and in 92% of these the residents earn zero income.

Post-Colonial Society / Immigrant Society

AMONG THOSE IN THE IRISH LITERARY pantheon, James Joyce is hardly alone in leaving: perhaps William Butler Yeats and Seamus Heaney (both Nobel Prize winners) are the only major exceptions (though as a teacher at Harvard, even Heaney lived part-time in the U.S. for many years). John Banville, too, we may credit with staying. As for Samuel Beckett, George Bernard Shaw, Oscar Wilde, Edna O'Brien — they all got away, and we can't call any among them particularly shy when it comes to extolling the benefits of their expatriation. Beckett once remarked that he would take wartime France over peacetime Ireland any day. (Even Colm Tóibín is only a part-time native, spending a large portion of every year in New York.) And yet, how eagerly, how passionately and — it occurred to me on more than a few occasions in Dublin, how *desperately* — the Republic and its capital claims them all, especially Joyce.

It seems important to ask: What were all these great writers getting away *from*? And why does Dublin cling to and claim them, willfully overlooking their abandonment of the place itself? It's more than a matter of profiting from their names (though there is that).

In *Ireland: A History*, Thomas Bartlett traces the country's reshaping as an "emigrant society." As he outlines the constant mass emigrations that began in the wake of the potato famine devastation of 1845, he observes: "From the 1850s on, with the formation of an Irish nation abroad, the history of Ireland and the history of the Irish people decisively diverge, with profound consequences for both Ireland and the Irish."

Does any other western country have so strong a tradition of expatriation and so fractured and fractious a sense of cultural identity?

"This absolute requirement to preserve an emigrant society ... is the key driver of modern Irish history," writes Bartlett. And later: "The initial decision to leave Ireland was not really made, it was simply assumed."

Is it in light of this tradition of emigration/abandonment, then, that Dublin might be the shell of a place that it seemed to me to be? In other words, if Irish culture is a *culture abroad*, a culture separate from its country, is Dublin a regional husk of that culture, whose exponents, through the generations, have largely remained in exile? Is that why Joyce and all the others had to go?

One can't blame the waves of emigrants for escaping. They've always had good reason. They started off in flight from famine, one million of them (nearly 13% of Ireland's population) in the space of the seven years between 1845 and 1852. And as author and archivist

Catriona Crowe explained in a lecture I attended at Trinity College, Dublin itself always contained Europe's worst slums, even while considered the "second city" of Great Britain and, prior to 1916, a "jewel" of the Empire. From 1919 on, the country was embroiled in war, first the War of Independence, and then — in the wake of the 1921 Anglo-Irish Treaty that split the country between home rule and British rule — in outright civil war that would last, through various brutal iterations, for roughly 77 years.

Misuse

"Ireland has the record for the most incarcerated children of the 20th century."
  —Catriona Crowe, lecturing, Trinity College

ONE MORNING WHILE IN DUBLIN, I set out early to visit a Cork-born Catholic priest in the city's southwest. Father Colin is an old family friend in his mid-eighties and served 17 years as a missionary in the Gambia, Liberia, and Sierra Leone. I found him in his modest, sparsely appointed apartment in a clerical retirement home that adjoins a college seminary. From his windows on the second floor there was a clear view of the Wicklow Hills, through which I would travel later that same day on a sojourn to the ancient monastic settlement of Glendalough. Father

Colin, nine-months along in recovery from major spinal surgery that he described as "unsuccessful," sat with apparent discomfort in an adjustable office chair, while I sipped coffee in an armchair facing him. As we talked, he told me that he pines for Africa, feels he still belongs there, though his missionary service ended well over twenty years ago due to a serious malarial infection. In his many years of unwilling residence back in Ireland, he has worked on the issue of the wellbeing of children, and is an executive of the Irish watchdog commission called The National Board for Safeguarding Children in the Catholic Church. But we did not talk of these things directly, and I sensed in the room a sober awkwardness that had something to do with the self-imposed devastation of the Catholic church's credibility in Ireland following the 2009 Ryan Report, the seismic moral and existential collapse of an institution to which this man has devoted his life.*

At one point, while sharing my thoughts about Dublin, I tried to describe my impressions of the somberness of the place, the darkness and troubles of its history. Father Colin listened and then, with the cold and righteous disgust of a person who has spent so

---

* A government-sponsored investigation begun in 1999 yielded the 2009 Ryan Report, a blistering public account of the systematic abuse, since 1936, of children housed in Ireland's church-run residential/educational institutions. The Report made clear not only the horrific and protracted extent of the abuses, but the role of Catholic Church leadership in endorsing and hiding these practices.

many years in service to the poor and vulnerable, replied: "Well, there's certainly been enough misuse of people here."

This hardworking man of the cloth, in whom the love of the Gambia is still so vivid — he too is firmly a part of Ireland's emigrant tradition. Garbed in sweater and slacks, he sat hunched in his own physical pain, wide awake to the depredations of his country's long history, and also, it seemed to me, alert to his own status as an old man marooned in this hollow place.

We Are No Petty People

"In a postcolonial society, everything is political."
—Dr. Conor McNamara, during a tour

WHILE THINKING OVER MY CONVERSATION with Father Colin as I rode the LUAS light-rail back to central Dublin that morning, I found myself reflecting on this year's centennial of the 1916 Rising — and the pains the Dublin organizers have taken to refer to the innumerable events, exhibitions, publications, conversations, and commentaries as *commemoration*, not "celebration." This is heartening and brave and right. It bodes well for Ireland, for its capital, and for the future of its people that they've embraced the dawning recognition of the damages wrought, through multiple generations, by once-heroic-seeming ideology and militant patriotism. The lie and waste of violent nationalism can now, perhaps, be put behind them at last. And perhaps, too, with that lie can be laid to rest all the ways in which endless political violence drains a culture of its vitality. For, as Seamus Heaney described in his 1995 Nobel lecture, the personal/political pressures of a militant atmosphere are pressures exerted on *sensibility*. In a violently nationalist climate, he said,

> Without needing to be theoretically instructed, consciousness quickly realizes that it is the site of variously contending discourses. The child in the bedroom, listening simultaneously to the domestic idiom of his Irish home and the official idioms of the British broadcaster while picking up from behind both the signals of some other distress, that child was already being schooled for the complexities of his adult predicament, a future where he would have to adjudicate among promptings variously ethical, aesthetical, moral, political, metrical, skeptical, cultural, topical, typical, post-colonial, and, taken all together, simply impossible.

Seven decades before Heaney's lecture, on a June day

in Dublin in 1925, Senator William Butler Yeats
delivered a courageous speech in the Parliament of the
newly established Irish Free State, a speech that
addressed what he saw as the persistent zealotry of
nationalist ideology. Yeats was by then an eminent poet
whose own work, so instrumental in the Irish cultural
revival, had inflamed the patriotic passions of several
younger poets who went on to spearhead the Rising.
But Yeats himself, the author of the powerful poetic
monument, "Easter, 1916," was always, at best,
ambivalent about the militancy with which Irish
independence was sought. "A terrible beauty is born,"
he writes in that famous poem. To his mind, the
"beauty" of independence won on the ground of
nationalistic violence could not be less than "terrible."
"Was it needless death after all?" he asks, referring to
the martyred leaders of the Rising. "...And what if
excess of love / Bewildered them till they died?"

On June 11, 1925, Senator Yeats stood up, ostensibly
to voice his objection to the outlawing of divorce in
Ireland. In fact he took the opportunity to address a
much more fundamental issue in the newly self-
governing country: the increasingly virulent divisions
between Anglo-Irish Protestants and the militant
nationalists who sought to establish a Catholic state. In
the course of his speech Yeats built up to a thunderous
defense of Anglo-Irish culture, locating himself firmly
within that milieu:

I think it is tragic that within three years of
this country gaining its independence we
should be discussing a measure which a
minority of this nation considers to be
grossly oppressive. I am proud to consider
myself a typical man of that minority. We,
against whom you have done this thing, are
no petty people. We are one of the great
stocks of Europe. We are the people of Burke;
we are the people of Grattan; we are the
people of Swift, the people of Emmet, the
people of Parnell. We have created the most
of the modern literature of this country. We
have created the best of its political
intelligence. Yet I do not altogether regret
what has happened. I shall be able to find out,
if not I, my children will be able to find out
whether we have lost our stamina or not. You
have defined our position and have given us a
popular following. If we have not lost our
stamina then your victory will be brief, and
your defeat final, and when it comes this
nation may be transformed.

Reading over a transcript of these Senate
proceedings, it astonished me to find so early and
impassioned an expression of affiliation to the cultural
traditions of the erstwhile colonizing power, England.
By Yeats's lights, in throwing out the English
overlords Ireland should take care not to throw out the

best of its own culture as well.

As it happened, of course, the ideological divisions that he was addressing persisted for the next 70-plus years and kept Ireland mired in a state of ongoing political violence and civil war.

Did these divisions, also, steadily empty Dublin of some of its cultural vitality, a precedent first set when young poets turned to warfare?

"You talk to me of nationality, language, religion," says Stephen Dedalus in Joyce's *A Portrait.* "I shall try to fly by those nets." In other words, Dedalus — and by extension, Joyce — will act freely and consciously as an agent of culture, outside of ideology. And, also, necessarily away from the stultifying environment of his native Ireland.

Absolutely Imagined

SEVENTY YEARS AFTER YEATS'S SENATE SPEECH, Seamus Heaney stood on the dais in Stockholm describing the difficulty of his early career, of having grown up in Northern Ireland, and of "having to conduct oneself as a poet in a situation of ongoing political violence and public expectation. A public expectation, it has to be said, not of poetry as such but of political positions variously approvable by mutually disapproving groups."

Heaney went on to elucidate his own unflagging faith

in "the sufficiency of that which is absolutely imagined," the capacity of poetry to "retune the world itself," to be "true to the impact of external reality and ... sensitive to the inner laws of the poet's being."

There are resonances here — historical, political, cultural — with Joyce's pledge to "forge in the smithy of my soul the uncreated conscience of my race," and with Yeats's urgings to preserve the best of culture even amid political restructuring. The collapse of Soviet totalitarianism, Heaney pointed out, came not through armed force but "was caused, among other things, by the sheer persistence, beneath the imposed ideological conformity, *of cultural values and psychic resistances.*" Heaney dared to suggest that similar values could likewise overwhelm, for good, the draining forces of ideological divisions in Ireland. He envisioned "a future where the vitality that flowed in the beginning from those bracing words 'enemy' and 'allies' might finally derive from a less binary and altogether less binding vocabulary." He was talking about the resurgence of *cultural* vitality.

Heaney concluded by affirming how poetry — that vitalizing force — "satisfies the contradictory needs which consciousness experiences at times of extreme crisis, the need on the one hand for a truth telling that will be hard and retributive, and on the other hand, the need not to harden the mind to a point where it denies its own yearnings for sweetness and trust."

Heaney was daring to avow, finally, that the Irish

people could bring about this cultural renewal at home,
no exile required.

Coda:
Notes Sketched After Visiting the Prehistoric Burial Sites
of Loughcrew and the Hill of Tara, and the National
Museum of Ireland's Bog Bodies, July 2016

"The whole of the Irish landscape is a manuscript which
we have lost the skill to read."
—Seamus Heaney, quoting John Montague

At Tara it is said: *And the stone cried out under his
feet*   And at Loughcrew, in the earthen
dark, of the earthen green and gray in the
innermost chambers of the cairn, the sun is a carving in
stone
       Out on the hilltop the scene all cloudshot, driven
in green, the stones jut against the overabundant blue
— not rocks so much as stones, these disintegrating
designators of all that you have loved, the chipped and
crumbling earthworks of something unearthly, your
leavings   Windblown. Of another time, gone
before — and gone   The inner passage isn't long,
but how deep the Neolithic resting place   How
deep   For here there were no approximates
    Those vanished people — their vanished octants
somehow factored the stars, the alignment of every

hour   And ours — our stars, that is — do we find
in that firmament this burrowing?   Wasn't it we
also who dug our caverns in the heavens then?

     We may not know what to make of the past

     But always, as we do know too well, time itself
imprints what's underfoot   Even now, the bog
people, mummified for millennia in Irish peat, and
latterly carried from the farmers' fields and laid behind
glass for visitors, remind us   There are no
approximates   How could there be?   The past,
those bygone ways, all the buried life, these things are a
mystery, but always the *forms* of the mystery — the
stacked rocks and bog-embalmed person — are
surprisingly exact   School-children, darting
through the museum, stop and press their hands
against the glass   Their looking is a kind of hope.

iii. Dryland, Dreamland (Andalucía Variations, 2017)

E N ROUTE TO GRANADA — landscape growing gradually hilly, then mountainous, the hard rocky ground thoroughly cultivated all the same with rows upon rows of low-standing trees

Stopped in Andalucían university city of Jaén for refreshments around 2:30, found ourselves in massive mall (Centro Commercial) complete with enormous supermarket   Sandwiches, sushi, café con leche

Onward 60 kilometers or so to Granada, arriving around 5:00 PM   Maneuvered our way to train terminal to meet Rafa, our host   All smiles, laughs, self-deprecating English, warm & fulsome hospitality

Followed Rafa on his Vespa uphill into the old town & on through increasingly cobbled, increasingly narrow streets all bordered by tile-capped walls of white stucco   Rafa insisted on helping carry our luggage from the garage around the block to the flat — a gorgeous series of tiled rooms off an enclosed courtyard   Windows onto gardens lush with trumpet flowers, high cypresses, palms, leafy climbers

Tile roofs in the distance (& up close)   Rafa offered a thorough, ebullient orientation about

Granada's delights, overflowing with pride   He is a
born-&-raised Granadan & this was his childhood home
       7:00 to 10:00 PM — into the streets of this
breathtaking, dizzying, all-senses-afire place
    Dinner: pizza from a tiny panderia eaten in the Plaza
San Nicolas with a view of the Alhambra in horizontal
ambers of the sinking sun.

———

U P EARLY FOR THE ALHAMBRA   A fast-walk
down the spidery cobbled lane of the Albaicín (Moorish
Quarter) to the Plaza Nueva & up again along the steep
Palace Road to the Puerto del Vino
    Birds, cats, orange trees, roses, morning glories,
magnolias, swifts, bubbling fountains, arcing fountains,
splashing fountains, water channeled into marble-
floored courtyards along open rivulets running from all
four directions, intricate Arabic carvings in stone,
plaster, wood — dizzying & tranquil tilework —
Islamic clerestories — star-shaped projections of light
on brick & apricot-colored stone — ogival arches
everywhere, receding perspectives framed by multiple
thresholds — courtyards within courtyards —
fortifications within fortifications — layers upon layers
horizontal & vertical, layers upon layers historical,
layers upon layers material: stone, brick, marble,
mahogany, tile, stucco, leaf, column, bushel,

crenellation, stairway, slope, pool, arcade, chamber, garden enclosure, tower, path, stair, door, shutter, terrace, wall   Out into the Albaicín again, back up cobbled lanes to the flat.

———

T HE WEARY, HUNCHED, FRAZZLE-HAIRED MOTHER standing at midday in the Calle Tiña with an infant at her breast.

———

T HE SCRAWNY CATS OF THE ALHAMBRA are Abyssinian in character   Large-eared, small of stature, shy despite an air of entitled desperation, with spacious round eyes of the same green as the waters in the Courtyard of the Lions & in the upper gardens of the sultan's summer retreat   They are no doubt self-aware, knowing their own larger cousins, rendered in the tribute of carved white stone, receive such prominent seats hereabouts   They strut & trot, these actual half-feral felines, as if endowed, a princely sort, decorous & dignified even in matted or mottled coats which suggest breeding more bohemian than courtly   One of them crossed the coarse golden dirt of the midday courtyard below the foremost guard tower to sit before me as I nibbled at my palatially apportioned croissant & sipped a café con leche from a glass   She did not beg   She only enthroned herself on her bony haunches, sphinx-like, & watched Not a word, not even a swish of the tail

High above us both, from the small divots dug by their ancestors over centuries into the fortified stone walls, swifts deployed themselves like arrows, veered & arced, dove & climbed, screaked, twirled, returned, unharmed, having tinged the Andalucían blue even bluer, the stone more golden, the aromatic fruit of the orange trees more spherical, all things robustly three-dimensional   The little cat pretended they were not there & went on declining to beg.

————

THE MIDNIGHT CLANGOR OF BELLS in the far-off black of the valley, the commotion of goats or livestock. (Outside Ronda.)

————

RONDA   Such disorientation has come, since leaving Toledo, of so thoroughly recognizing the character & features of this Andalucían landscape

Its golds & greens   Its rocky dryness & ever-
shifting elevations   Even the situations of the lone
houses nestled here & there amid cypresses & palms
     The oaks, the chaparral, the brown craggy
mountains hazing off behind it all   Lemon trees,
pomegranate trees, pink oleander, white oleander
     The broad canopies of the oaks on the dry hillsides,
their disks of pure shade dotting the slopes   The
quality of ancient persistence in all these human
settlements of such a stony, crackling land —
humankind finding gardens where none have been
given — extracting from unyielding earth all the
necessary nutrients, then sustaining them despite the
unforgiving sun   Here they've had centuries upon
centuries of practice   No wonder, 250 years back,
California could not scare them   In their book of
millennia that was only yesterday, not even a chapter
prior, not even a page, perhaps a passing paragraph
Ronda, it is said, is one of the oldest cities in Spain
Yesterday's drive from Granada   2.5 hours,
blinding sunlight, blinding blue sky, blinding golds,
blinding crags all the way   Since Granada & our
perpetually confusing turnabouts in the dense &
aromatic Albaicín, our surroundings have induced,
more & more, the sensation of dreams   Elusive
familiarity   Impossible exoticism   A bedrock
of ancientness   And, within or behind it all, an
awareness of being watched: watched, somehow, by the
immutable surroundings themselves   The gardens

& courtyards of the Alhambra — of all the little (&
large) carmens of old Granada — an Edenic familiarity,
a storybook perspicacity about the place itself that is
almost biblical, all-seeing   (Do we travel so far to
see these old places, or rather to *be seen* by the places
themselves?)

The drive deeper into Andalucía was a drive, also,
into dream   As we never fail to *be recognized* in
dreams, so we seek those locales that will show us, in
waking life, that they see us   *How* they see us
Andalucía is a dream of this kind   It sees me

Lunch in Ronda's Mercadillo, a dense city all but
fast asleep in the late-day heat   We too were
sapped, weary, oversunned   But back in the car, we
found our way north of Ronda, across the broad valley,
along snaking country lanes amid haciendas, horse
farms, crumbling stone stables, derelict disowned
churches, to the end of the paved road & past that onto
gravel, to turn up a long single-track drive between
rowed cypresses, to this oasis-like hacienda on its
hilltop   Villa Casa Alta   Down the grassy
slope from the casa grande is our casita: two bedrooms,
a bathroom, a spare little kitchenette, a porch with a
view toward the north edge of Ronda, the Sierra
Nevada embracing the whole scene from the
background   Drive into Ronda 9:00 PM for dinner
& paseo   We find the Mercadillo newly alive &
wander amid the families & elderly folks toward the old
town Moorish quarter   The cliff-edge astounds,

the Puente Nueva stands true   We linger & gawk & nervously lean, stomachs aflutter at the sight   The precipitous stone walls of the gorge floodlit at twilight

Dinner perched on the canyon's edge with a view of the Puente Nueva from the Mercadillo side

Then back to Villa Casa Alta along unlit country roads all stone-black at midnight   The country a pure black, spangled with townlights, but more so with stars.

———

W E ARE IN A DRY LAND   We are in a dreamland We are in our homeland & it is nowhere near our home.

———

A S THE SPANIARDS, ARRIVING not so long ago, not so very long ago, named it anew, named it Alta California, having found it so familiar, having felt themselves recognized in the dryness of the land, having felt the land itself dreaming them, their very arrival a dream this dry land was dreaming, so I, as I drive these winding highways through the greens & golds of Andalucía, drive deeper into dream, until I too am only one figure dreamed by the dry land itself.

———

THE OLIVE TREE, ROOTED HERE in rock, in sun-blasted rock, is a kind of dream, but the dreamer is not the seed of the tree itself, & not the green fruit of the olive, nor the glistening oil crushed from the olive — no, the dreamer is the rock   And the olive stone, freed by teeth from its skin, sidled by tongue into pocket of cheek, bathed in golden oil, tinged in bitterness, finally spat into palm or plate, the olive stone, immutable, more closely embodies the dreaming rock than the edible fruit can ever do.

———

WE ARE IN A DRY LAND, dreaming   But it is we who are dreamed, & the land that is the dreamer.

———

OLD CITIES, OLD RONDA, one of the first in Spain — how else to interpret you, atop your immemorial gorge, but to notice how you levitate there, not exactly anchored to the far more ancient stone, nor soaring toward the more celestial, eternal — no, simply levitating — the very image of a dream, neither bound nor boundless, neither substantial nor immaterial   You are a gateway city Despite your fortifications, your purpose is passage,

permeation, threshold   Along your cliffsides we linger
& lean, looking down, looking up
    On the flung dream of your bridge we stand, or go
slow, like figures on a ship at sea   Far below, the
river winds along, a memory   But we are dreamed
    Everywhere we turn we find ourselves dreamt.

A<small>ND THE DREAMS THIS LAND DREAMS</small> are not dreams
of apotheosis   We are not a wish long harbored by
the land   The fig tree, the wheat field, the oleander,
the sturdy & resplendent oak, the hacienda, the railroad,
the fountain — the dreaming is underway always & these
are but signs & figures of the dreaming
    They are not themselves the dream.

T<small>HE LAND DOES NOT</small> *DESIRE*, whatever the marshal
or missionary creed may claim, in the Alta California of
1775 or elsewhere, else*when*.

WE ARE IN OUR HOMELAND   It is nowhere
near our home   But the golds, the blinding blue, &
the untold memory of rock enfold us   Ronda on its
hill   These barren mountains that Rilke read like an
open psalter   That white house far across the valley,
standing amid clustered cypresses   Go on dreaming
   Dream me, my memories, everything I love.

———

SEVILLA   Flamenco: the wrists & fingers of the
dancers constantly plucking fire from the sun
   The male dancer strutting slowly across the length of
the stage — in search of the music's burning soul
   The seriousness, the playfulness, the joy, the intensity,
the mystery   the dream ...

iv. The Birthplace (Salzburg Variations, 2022)

IN THE MOZART GEBURTSHAUS (the birthplace) the
low-ceilinged rooms remain   Each doorway is
small   Here are collected the requisite
oddments, the artifacts, a few belongings and effects:
letters, scores, sketches, and portraits   Most are
facsimiles, and this is fitting   The man is not to be
found, not here nor in the rooms of a second lesser
shrine across the river (the later family home)

————

THE WINDOWS of this birthplace give onto a market
square and the imposing front of Holy Trinity Church
   The windows frame a picture little changed these last
three centuries   The sills receive the timeless
sunlight, ancient church shadow, music of the bell
towers, voices bustling from stalls below, heat wind
rain and snow — all this is the same
        and it speaks no one's particular name   The
man is not to be found in these rooms that never
sufficed (like the town that never sufficed) to hold him

ENSHRINED SPOT-LIT IN LONG CAPSULES of glass are
the buttons of a dress coat, a finely crafted tobacco box,
a silken wallet   And yes, these things belonged,
like the locks of hair here also enshrined, to a man who
wore coats, who carried money, who enjoyed his pipe
and wigs   But he cannot belong to them
　　In them the man is not to be found

EVEN THE CLAVICHORD displayed here, accompanied
with plaque explaining which musical works emerged
as he sat at its keys (the *Requiem* among them) — even
this clavichord does not astonish, surprisingly small
though it is   Of course it doesn't
　　For the visitor knows that no single instrument
gave rise to the music   That was mind's work
　　heart's work   And at these narrow keys the
man is not to be found

UPON A WALL the visitor reads *Nach Leben* —
"posterity," or literally "afterlife"   And a sketch

represents the physiognomy of the Mozart ear — an
ear peculiarly enlarged, they say   This too cannot
make clear or explain   The man is not in the ear
    The living mind of the music alone: that's the only
feasible afterlife

———

N OW I'VE FOUND MY WAY BACK across the river
        time's river and river of sound, memory's river
and river of pilgrimage, river of listening and afterlives
—   to the little Friedhof in the courtyard of San
Sebastian   Here I've stood a while before the
father's grave   stern miracle maker Leopold
Mozart   and the grave of Constanze   Mozart's
devoted spouse and memory builder   I've brought
my thanks to them both, both who are very much to be
found in this place   Music maker, these were his
music givers   They created conditions propitious
to the opening of ears — maybe his ears first of all
    For *it is the nature of music to be ongoing*   and the
listening precedes the composing, always the listening

———

B UT IF THE MAN HIMSELF is not to be found   If,
searching, the visitor finds him nowhere around, let's
remember the reasons, all of which the music provides:

the tones flowing forward through time, flowing
forever, maybe   *it is the nature of music to be ongoing*
  The man is hardly a man at all but becomes a
cosmos of sound

———

B<small>Y NIGHTFALL</small> this side of the river I stream up a
marbled staircase festooned with cherubim
    I enter a marbled music hall to hear the
very sounds, to witness walls and high coffered ceiling
awakening to that cosmos again It's said that he
played this room in his time But still the man is
not to be found Here too he has stepped aside, put
himself out of the way Yet he's left the windows
open to the summer night that never ends
    Through the windows the tones flow forward,
forward through time allegro time andante time
presto time the player's strings clacking against
the necks of their instruments He's put himself
out of the way but this is the one and only *Nach Leben*
language language larger than his name I
and my fellow listeners, motionless in our seats, flow
forward through time until the time arrives to leave the
hall time to join together in the prosaic procession
    out into night, unmusical as it seems And is
the man to be found among us? Having listened,
infused with minuetto time and scherzo time and
presto, we leave the hall But what is left in the

hall as we go?   And who among us will see the hall
again?   *It is the nature of music to be ongoing*

———

WALKING SALZBURG'S MOONLIT STREETS,
rounding a corner, coming past the San Sebastian bell
tower, some of us notice scaffolds encasing the church
      A new copper roof is going in up there   It
glimmers   And we, glimmering too, stand a
minute, this once in a few centuries, to consider the
sight   Destined to take its classic patina, tonight
it's as pink as a newly minted penny
      How long until it's green?

BOOK THREE:
Is there any such thing as a complete and finished story?

It took the dark forever to do its job, and we saw no cause to fear its arrival. The evening had brought it, after all, leading it home with us like a woman on its arm, letting her go ahead at the door.

Self-Portrait in a Convex Mirror
Francesco Mazzola, 1523/24

"After arriving in Rome the young artist presented a self-portrait painted on a convex piece of wood to Pope Clement VII, hoping thus to gain a great patron who would commission works from him. Despite the modest format and limited range of colors, the concept was extremely clever and the artistic demands were very high: the deliberate confusion between reflection and original image are [sic] in keeping with the spirit of modern painting at the time, which focused on deception and illusion."
—placard, Kunsthistorisches
Museum, Vienna

The boy is enbubbled   He's put himself there   He's only a boy   The portrait is mirror and lens alike   He's

looking at you   or his likeness is   through glass he's
implied but hasn't painted   The portrait is a projection
    a broadcast   not only will you see him   he will
make himself seen

    Lay it on me, the delicious insatiable lens   I am he,
the one you see, self and self-advertisement   My room
distorts behind me: its upward stretching walls, its
demented windowsill warping into view   My hand,
which fashioned this, swells in the foreground   my
head diminishing   Distortion is the deal   the
unspoken guarantee   part of the joke maybe   You will
see what I want you to see and be well-pleased

    Delirium I deliver   Spectacle I supply, an
astonishment of my making   Ensphered, I send my
image to you   Ensphered you receive it   Can we wish
for much beyond this?   Can a sphere ever touch
another sphere beyond a single point?

    Foreshortening, elongation, elaboration, illusion,
embellishment   What if the entire visual world were a
fiction?   What if we admitted it?   I play, you play, and
here is the record of this reiteration   Irresponsible and
grave   Sincere and slippery   Performative and
plangent   Beautiful and shameless   Open-handed

    Open-eyed   This portrait itself an eye   the convex
of my own eye seeing me, I am seeing me in order to
send me to you   Resize and crop   Here I come across
the airwaves   a visual transmission from a satellite that
passed 500 years back   It's brief, it's bold   if you blink
you may miss it   but it's the best I can do   Will you

have me?   Do you want this?   What will you make of
what I've made for you?   Either way, it is on its way to
you   And funny to see, after these five centuries, that
you are no stranger to the broadcast
    Let's look at one another   porthole and porthole
aligned   Let's peer from the bubble   lensed and
convex   and find one another amid the stimuli   My
time, your time   they just might mean the same thing.

You, Me, and the Screen Between

1.

W E THOUGHT IT WAS A WINDOW. We stared at it, the screen, believing we looked through it to something larger.

Early on, the images arrived as light projections: reels of film enlarged on a wall. Later, they were signals transmitted via airwaves to electron beams and cathode ray tubes. Still later, we turned to digital transmission and LED display.

The screen diverted our attention. We found it soothing at day's end. It also exacerbated our anxieties constantly. We came to accept our new and queasy agitation.

From the newsreel evolved the nightly news, evolved hourly updates, evolved minute-to-minute tweets. We tried and failed to absorb the never-ending flood of images.

We were told the screen gave us the wide world in our living rooms, and we watched as world events swelled to an exponential scale and number, while the screen, our means of delivery, shrank to pocket-size. Soon the screen was giving us, with shocking clarity, an instantaneousness seeming to verge on something sublime.

The screen received our devotion, a fixed attention we'd formerly reserved for religious icons, or for our work as artists, journalists, educators, naturalists, philosophers. It provided an immediate access to others that was purported to defy all distance, even as it steadily reduced the time we spent face to face and in conscious proximity to one another.

It gave us each an "@" of our own. It gave us the shortest route, the time of the next train or bus, the way with the least amount of walking. It gave us the powers to reserve and to book, gave us "social," gave us "streaming," gave us "interactive."

As our late Librarian of Congress Daniel Boorstin observed of technology generally, the screen quickly multiplied our needs for unnecessary things and increased our involuntary commitments.* It seemed to demand that we each constantly remind the world of our existence, our likes and dislikes, our delight and outrage.

The screen and its delivery devices gave us the notion of the "upgrade" and its corollary: planned obsolescence on an unthinkable scale. It gave us our coordinates from outer space, while numbing us to the immediacy of the geo-physical moment that enfolded us. All the while, our landfills accumulated silicon and mercury and mountains of plastic, glass, and copper waste.

---

* See Boorstin's "The Republic of Technology and the Limits of Prophecy"

Enthralled by the screen, we came to question the necessity of privacy. We learned to let go of old values, and to require speed, convenience, portability, connectivity. We learned to desire our stats and the stats of others. We learned to accept the special way the screen reduced to equivalencies all things seen within its frame: NASCAR, cop shows, TV journalism, late night comedians, cat GIFS, and the office of the presidency. Gone was the idea of everything in its proper place. More screen, less "meatspace" and IRL. More optimization, less serendipity. More jump-cuts, less syntax. More data, data, data. More info, info, info. We embraced the self-promoting capacities and tools the screen promised us. We learned to expect an audience. We honed the skill of performing our lives in lieu of merely living them.

The screen created the "sharing economy," the "attention economy," the "gig economy," and a special iteration of the "creative class" — a brave new world in which it seemed that everybody's individual passion had, at long last, converged with their livelihood, while in fact hardly anybody was making a living anymore.

The screen provided us 2,000 songs in the palm of the hand but dealt a fatal blow to the solvency of musicians. The screen provided the texts of 3,500 books at a weight of 9.5 ounces but contributed to the dissolution of publishers and booksellers and weakened the infrastructure that supported and sustained authors.

The screen empowered and accelerated the mobilization of righteous movements: the Arab Spring and Occupy Wall Street and the Million Women March and Black Lives Matter, but it exposed us as never before to the rapacity of advertisers, to the invasive scrutiny of our own government agencies under the PATRIOT Act, to a massive blurring of private and professional life, to the political meddling of extra-national bots, to the daily specter of harassment by anonymous trolls, and to amplified terrorist threats both international and domestic.

Our fixation on the screen forged new neural networks and sharpened into biochemical habit our reluctance toward the printed page, our acceptance of incoherent audio-visual stimuli, and our need to fictionalize our lives not only for others but publicly for ourselves.

The screen led us away from the book toward the illumined mirage, away from ideas toward memes.

The screen gave us new meanings: desktop, window, home, field, friend.

It redefined everything.

———

2.

NOW, HERE IN THE MADDING WAKE of the 45th American presidency, let us remember that once upon a time we impeached the screen. TV itself was made to stand trial before the U.S. Congress. The memories are hazy, the details obscured as if behind a veil of snowy static, but this happened. America, a land of electronic images, big pharma, high-tech distraction, and endless advertising, seemed to be teetering on the cusp of an awful new reality. False impressions were the stock in trade, big onscreen metrics mattered most, and in the midst of this a white man played a version of himself on primetime. He was a celebrity and a winner, and he ruled the ratings.

The object of this man's game was to claim knowledge he didn't possess, and to provide an image viewers would anxiously fixate upon and maybe even idolize. He was a man more closely watched than any person of any time before him. He became TV and TV became him.

The year was 1956. The program was a quiz show called *Twenty-One*. The man was Charles Van Doren, a thirty-year-old intellectual and aspiring novelist who taught literature at Columbia. His father was a Pulitzer Prize-winning poet, his uncle a Pulitzer Prize-winning biographer, and his mother an erstwhile editor of *The Nation* magazine.

Between November 1956 and March 1957 Charlie
Van Doren scored repeated victories on *Twenty-One*,
becoming this country's hottest star, and racking up
cash winnings of $129,000 — more than a cool million
today. Eventually, though, the illusion broke and a
spellbound nation awakened to a rude truth, when
Charlie and his fellow quiz show contestants were outed
as fakes: they'd all been supplied answers ahead of time,
enabling *Twenty-One*'s producers to maximize drama
and pump up audience numbers. This scheme had sent
sales of sponsors' products — pharmaceuticals mostly
— through the roof.

Americans watched, unblinking, as Charlie's screen-
image and Charlie's real self diverged horribly. Into the
chasm between icon and individual flooded a repulsive
reality. Charlie was a lie, and for months upon months
the screen had beamed the lie right into hearth and
home.

Would America stand for this? No. On behalf of a
defrauded public the U.S. Congress intervened. Charlie
was called to testify before a House subcommittee.
Rumpled, haggard, and humiliated, he was sworn in,
took his seat, and read out a statement bemoaning his
part in the sordid chapter.

In our various retellings of this national story
throughout the last several decades, we've tended to
frame the quiz show scandals as a seminal loss of
"American innocence" at the hands of our first great
media manipulators, a cadre of unscrupulous, skinny-

tied TV producers and their ad-man accomplices. It was a top-down scam, and the moral seemed clear: watch out for bamboozlers and molders of the public mind. Maybe you've heard that story.

But hang on a minute. If we look at Van Doren's congressional statement now, today, in the noisome heat and roar of our own disinformed, conspiracy-theory-drenched heyday, what's immediately striking is Charlie's phrasing. About his sweat-soaked TV performances, when he stood locked in his glass isolation booth and pretended to grope for answers he already knew, Charlie told the committee:

> I was deeply troubled by the arrangement. As time went on, the show ballooned beyond my wildest expectations. From an unknown college instructor, I became a celebrity. I was almost able to convince myself that it did not matter what I was doing because it was having such a good effect on the national attitude to teachers, education, and the intellectual life. I was able to convince myself that I could make up for it after it was over.

Twice he says here: *I was able to convince myself.* And elsewhere in his testimony: *I persuaded myself.*

———

CHARLES VAN DOREN had been born to a clan of
literarians and scholars who publicly extolled disciplined
thought, lucid expression, and the examined life. His
father, Mark Van Doren, had hosted *Invitation to
Learning*, an old CBS Radio panel show featuring
intellectuals in unhurried discussion of Aristotle, Pascal,
Lucretius, Tacitus, Dante, Milton. And here was Charlie
admitting surrender to the sleazy, factitious spectacle of
TV. S*urrender*, not bamboozlement. In other words, by
his own account Charlie had *talked himself* into accepting
the warped logic of the small screen. This logic is still
centrally operative on the myriad screens we cling to
today: *Rewards come to those who fake.* Charlie was saying
he'd bought into this. He was saying: My Faustian
bargain was with myself alone.

The point about these long-ago TV scandals, a point
mostly missed in post-mortems ever since, is not that
powerful interests shamelessly perpetrated a national
fraud. The point is that we saw a profound
epistemological shift in American culture. As Lionel
Trilling (the great literary critic who was a colleague of
the Van Dorens at Columbia) wrote in his 1972
book *Sincerity & Authenticity*: "The deception we best
understand and most willingly give our attention to is
that which a person works upon himself." Ensnared by
television, Charlie had deceived *himself*, and at the height
of the quiz show boom, millions upon millions of people
like and unlike him participated, from living rooms all

across America, in a new and special kind of self-deception induced by the spectacularly alluring electronic screen. This was an end-user issue. Already back then, the enthralled populace watching Charlie's TV conquest was wondering how one could so glamorously optimize a self for broadcast: *Am I smart enough? Good-looking enough? Likeable enough? Can I fake it when I need to? Am I convincing?*

It was the young Van Doren's ethereal performance and everything the performance projected — more than any singular quality of the man himself — that so mesmerized the viewer at home. His clean, coolly black-and-white *screeniness* made him an avatar every viewer longed to inhabit. The magical question was: How do you make yourself into an image like that?

Given this telegenic wonder of the quiz show, it hardly mattered whether the game and its players were for real. Throughout the national *Twenty-One* craze many of the show's avid fans, surveyed by the press, admitted that they didn't entirely buy the events onscreen, and for most this scarcely dimmed their enjoyment. "Everything on TV is somewhat of a lie," one of them remarked in a straw poll by the *Miami Herald*, "but it's still entertainment."

One week before coming clean to Congress, Charlie graced the cover of *Life* magazine. Inside those pages, everyday viewers were asked their opinions on the unfolding scandal. A "New York salesgirl" stated she'd rather not know the shows were fixed, adding, "If the contestants were not OK, at least the answers were." The scandal left another young New Yorker unfazed: "So what? I still think that those guys were smart." Other respondents shruggingly acknowledged the stupefying power of primetime: "We're going to go right on watching." "Television interests people no matter what happens." The *seeming*, not the *being*, was the irresistible point. It's a short metaphysical distance from there to the solipsistic koan so many of us now live by: *If I'm alone, if I'm unseen, if I'm off-screen, do I exist?* To *appear* — and to be dependably visible and available for admiration — is the whole game.

In the years to come, that small screen would give Americans much more than they'd bargained for: the JFK assassination, the Vietnam War, Nielsen ratings, the OJ Simpson trial, Reality TV, and the forty-fifth president of the United States.

3.

CHARLES VAN DOREN WAS BRILLIANT and capable, but ultimately a sad figure whose early self-deception seemed to become his lifelong shame. He never escaped the shadow of the quiz show scandals, but lived out of the public eye, occasionally authoring books. He died in 2019. It's hard not to think that he might have been the perfect person, in his later years, to speak to the long and continual reverberations of the quiz show scandals in our visual media culture. Today, even though we claim to understand the dramatic ways television redefined American life, we each fiddle endlessly with our own pocket-sized screen. Amassing "likes" and "friends," we each possess an audience, we know our stats, and so we're given a devilishly efficient means of quantifying our life experience and rating our onscreen performances. Social life and showmanship, community and game show-like competition have blurred entirely. Our rankings are public. Who has the highest score on Facebook, on Twitter, on Instagram? We seem to think this contest can be won.

The quiz show riggings, culminating in Charlie Van Doren's ashamed statement to Congress, were the beginning of a techno-cultural remodeling of self and society that has never let up. Our bizarre democratic breakdowns today — breakdowns of discourse, of factual consensus, of civic commonality, of legislative process — are directly related to those half-forgotten events. Back then, the small screen broadcast rigged game shows, and more recently it projected a facsimile of competence and power on *The Apprentice* seasons one through fourteen. Now it disseminates social media amusement, conspiracy theories, and outrage. At every point, overwhelmingly, the screen has drawn us toward the reductive or outright false: counterfeit visions and counterfeit selves in various video permutations.

Today, with facts more universally accessible than ever before in history, it is not a top-down bamboozlement that got us to our current place of ideological entrenchment, vicious mutual mistrust, and simmering citizen-to-citizen violence, but rather the decision, made millions and millions of times over *by individuals* across the country, to bamboozle the self. Most of us are skilled in the same web-enabled tools of self-delusion and self-aggrandizement used so feverishly by our recently departed, twice-impeached president. A white male celebrity whose identity is inextricable from TV, he embraced viral falsehoods and unflaggingly enunciated lies: e.g., *The election was stolen!* But he was only modeling, albeit with devastating ferocity and consequence, impulses that are alive in all of us, and which our screen-centered technologies intensify. The screen, which seemed at first to give us the wide world, now gives us nothing so much as image after image of our increasingly narrow selves. This thing we believed to be a window is a distorted mirror. In the 45th president we had a man whose endless fraud was not the product of brilliant calculation but a trademark of delusional screen addiction. His every action was motivated by the screen and his need to reflect there an enviable and commanding person. This man troubles us deeply because his actions and words are so often corrosive, yes, but also because we recognize in him our own surrender to the falsity and narcissism of the screen-mind. We all know a little too well that pathology of posing, of performing a "self" for our own eyes as much as anyone's. The 45th president was our self-deceiver in chief.

He also troubles us because he appears incapable of recognizing the damage he and his sycophants are wreaking upon our democratic norms and institutions. For his direct incitement of the January 6th violence he should be held responsible, just like the rioters who invaded the capitol. And social media companies — whose algorithms served to accelerate the lies and hate of violent agitators and endanger democracy in the interest of ad revenue — should be regulated. But let's awaken to the fact that every one of us, living online as we do, is vulnerable to screen-induced self-deception, a massively amplified form of our more natural self-delusional propensities. Your screen is buzzing for your attention right now, urging you to claim your audience: YouTube wants you to "broadcast yourself" and Facebook asks "do you want to boost this post?" and someone just shared a tweet that mentions you, and 113 people *like* your video.

In its insanity, January 6th 2021 offered a dangerously real image of our screen-mind at the extremes. From those quaintly transfixing quiz shows of the late 1950s to our current moment, the trajectory is clear. Outlandishly costumed, confused, murderous, and festooned with hateful symbols as they smashed and stalked their way through the corridors of the U.S. capitol and into the Senate chamber, that day's rioters, urged on by the president's rhetoric, went charging toward their own self-induced delusion in video overdrive. Using the same devices with which they'd cultivated the delusion, now they were out to capture their starring roles in a cinéma vérité action movie. Would it be a hostage thriller? A shootout? The bloody birth of a new republic? Would they die onscreen? It hardly mattered, as long as it was streamed live or uploaded for a like-minded audience of "friends" and followers watching expectantly from home.

It's crucial that we realize what monstrous things we bring into being, individually and collectively through our devices, when we persist in deceiving ourselves for performative ends.

Scherzo: Glossary of Spectacle & Bewilderment (with Anecdotes) Compiled on Behalf of the Imaginative Mind

"The writer is the person who has not been dominated by someone else's vocabulary."
  —Adam Phillips, *Promises, Promises*

adaptation (book to film or book to limited series) Considered the aim of all literature, any book's apotheosis.

(Does a thing exist if it can't be played on a screen?)
Antonym: *literature.*
See MOVIES.

A.I. "Artificial Intelligence," an oxymoronic locution; stems from the logical fallacy that makes people liken silicon chips with human neurons.

Discussions about A.I., sometimes fretful and sometimes ecstatic, are generally short-sighted, relying upon a distorted denotation in the word "intelligence," i.e., intelligence conceived as a phenomenon reducible to functions but also synonymous with consciousness. And yet consciousness is irreducible.

Dramatic predictions about A.I.'s destined societal and cultural role almost always originate in faulty syllogisms concerning brains and electricity.

To wit, Syllogism A:

> Computer memory operates by electrical
> signals that are reducible to mathematical
> algorithms, *and* ... Electrical signals are
> the reducible basis of human intelligence,
> *therefore* ... A computer using mathematic-
> cal algorithms can replicate human
> intelligence!

Similar mystifications and conflations occur around
the question of whether computers will one day,
somehow, acquire consciousness and become sentient.
Therefore, Syllogism B:

> Networks take on attributes of adaptation
> similar to those in humans, *and* ... Human
> attributes of adaptation are the basis of
> consciousness, *therefore* ... Computer
> networks will acquire consciousness!

Or, Syllogism C:

> A.I. software's algorithmic pattern
> recognition acquires linguistic skill, which
> is essential to human consciousness,
> although the human brain's capacity to
> recognize linguistic patterns is
> physiologically limited, *and* ... A.I.
> software has no such limitations, *therefore*

... A.I. software's infinite linguistic
pattern recognitions will eventuate in
consciousness superior to humans!

But of course language, electrical signals, and basic
pattern recognition, if essential to human sentience, are
not all that constitutes it. Language patterns replicated
by machine may seem to replicate consciousness, but
only *seem*, e.g., automated semantic aping. Among the
most zealous technorati, the real neurological
permutations, psychic purposes, and metaphysical
mysteries of human memory, dream, Id/Ego, creativity,
intuition, and imagination, etc., are routinely — and
obscenely — reduced in false technological
equivalencies. Meanwhile, for Tristan Harris, founder of
the Center for Humane Technology, A.I. of a banal but
diabolical kind "already runs today's world, right now,"
— that is, through ubiquitous online software — and its
effects amount to "human downgrading."

Antonym: *consciousness*.

See ALGORITHM; AUGMENTED REALITY;
DEEP FAKE; DYNAMOS.

(One of my second-term Composition students turns
in an essay on James Baldwin sneakily generated by a
so-called chatbot. The bloodless writing immediately
betrays the source. It's a litter-pile of inexpressive
language — hackneyed pseudo-literary-analytical terms
harvested from an auto search of the Web. Nowhere to
be found is the stamp of insight that characterizes a

human response to literature. Most students, whatever their skill level, write better than this [because more humanly].

Consider, as a far cry from the robotic myopia and rigidity of computer "intelligence," John Ruskin's description of the *creative human intelligence.* "Imagine," says Ruskin, "all that any of these [creative souls] had seen or heard in the course of their lives, laid up accurately in their memories as in vast storehouses — extending with the poets even to the slightest intonations of syllables heard in the beginnings of their lives, and with the painters down to the minute folds of drapery and shapes of loaves or stones — and over all this unindexed and immeasurable mass of treasure the imagination brooding and wandering, but dream-gifted, so as to summon at any moment exactly such groups of ideas as shall justly fit each other: this I conceive to be the real nature of the imaginative mind."

Note how Ruskin's words capture the peculiarly powerful expressivity of the "brooding," "wandering," and "dream-gifted" human mind, all quintessential attributes to which the technocrat's concept of "intelligence" pays no heed. Machines and algorithms will never possess imagination and cannot experience inspiration or insight.

The problem with the vague deployment of the word "intelligence" amid our technocratic chatter is that, as Michael Ignatieff has said, "We are confused about what thinking is. To think is not to process information. We have impoverished our understanding of thinking by analogizing it to what our machines do. What we do is not processing. It is not computation. It is not data analysis. It is a distinctively, incorrigibly human activity that is a complex combination of conscious and unconscious, rational and intuitive, logical and emotional reflection. It is so complex that neither neurologists nor philosophers have found a way to model it, and the engineers of artificial intelligence are still struggling to replicate some of the simplest forms of pattern recognition that human cognition does so effortlessly. We must beware that in our attempt to make computers think like us we do not end up thinking like them."*)

algorithm A problem-solving procedure in mathematics, frequently involving repeated processes. Its more recent application in computer programming has made the term ubiquitous. As invoked today, "algorithm" carries a connotation of inevitability; i.e., increasingly we understand that our Zeitgeist — and firstly each of our individual states of mind — are algorithmically determined.

Antonym: *serendipity*.

See TECHNOPOLY.

(Clicking open Yahoo News, I skim an article about a

---

* From Ignatieff's "Epistemological Panic, or Thinking for Yourself," *Liberties* journal V.3 No.2

Hanta virus outbreak occurring in the guest cabins at Yosemite National Park. A few fatalities. Three or four days later, another Hanta virus story pops up in my Yahoo News headlines. Electronic reading is strictly determinant: whatever one reads on a web-connected screen determines the results the algorithm proffers next. In this case: I am offered an opportunity for paranoia under the guise of taking in "the news." One's algorithmically tailored newsfeed becomes one's worldview.

"We would do well," writes Garret Keizer in his profound little book *Privacy,* "to ask if the capitalist economy and its obsessions with smart marketing and technological innovation cannot become as intrusive as any authoritarian state.")

artist as kook A figure we know well — and who needs him? Enfant terrible, western but flamboyantly wears kimono, alcoholic (Truman Capote/Phillip Seymour Hoffman as); shoots big game, likes to fight (Ernest Hemingway/Clive Owen as); staggers around, barks at people (Beethoven/Gary Oldman as).

Antonym: *artist at work.*

(I couldn't resist watching the online trailer for the movie *Hemingway and Gellhorn.* In the span of ninety seconds, Clive Owen as Hemingway tosses back shots, dives for cover in wartime Spain, throws punches, screams at his woman, and initiates a round of double Russian roulette. I emailed a friend: "As bad as the

Hemingway myth is for a writer of my kind, rendering me a generally uninteresting wimp who likes to read and write books that contain compound sentences as well as the occasional adverb, and who abstains from smoking, drinking, hunting, womanizing, Russian roulette, going to war, and pounding furniture with my fists while I scream 'Get in the ring, Gellhorn!,' I still want to see that movie!")

augmented reality a.k.a. the Internet on your face!
Antonym: *reality*.
See FACEBOOK, etc.
(In elite circles Google rolled out, some time ago, prototypes of "Glass," high-fashion, Internet-enabled spectacles. An online video introducing Glass gave viewers a test drive behind the all-knowing lenses. Through the eyes of a young hipster in New York, we wake on a couch to find our lenses displaying data on the weather. The lenses alert us that subway service is suspended and supply a series of trusty arrows to guide us along an alternate walking route. We command the lenses to snap a photo of arresting graffiti art and upload it immediately to our social network. A video call comes in and we see our friend's face in our lower field of vision. We notice the sunset over Brooklyn and enable View Share to show friend exactly what our lenses see. "Wow, it's beautiful!" says friend.

The term "augmented reality" is typical of the utopian hyperbole long featured in the technocratic sphere. The message is clear: no self-respecting consumer would opt for the drab, anachronistic, woefully analog quotidian vision supplied by our own low-tech eyeballs — not when, for a modest monthly fee, all sights can come with data "enhancements." Unmediated life is so yesterday.

The "American way" is largely predicated upon a preference for changing our products rather than changing our behavior, in this case trying to change — "augment" — the way things look. And what if, instead, we changed *the way we look at things?*)

binge Formerly denoted behavior harmful to personal health, including excessive eating or drug and alcohol use. Formerly strongly associated with the disorder bulimia nervosa, which entails periods of self-induced vomiting and other purging following spells of excess. Still faintly retains (for the next fortnight or so) a residue of its original negative connotation — as "guilty pleasure." Subject not only to connotative but denotative distortions, "binge" increasingly indicates an approved action undertaken as a means of self-care; e.g., "It's been a long week, I'm going home to binge Season 3 of *Friends*, see you Monday."

Antonym: *moderation.*

See VIRAL.

cancellation (so-called) Specter as much as spectacle. A latter-day stocks or pillory, in which we subject a person to prolonged public shaming, often leading to the destruction of relationships and career. Like the stocks and pillory, the nature and intent of the punishment is to invite and exacerbate groupthink and mob tendencies. Invariably provokes ideological backlash from the opposing political camp (regardless of which "side" initiates the cancellation). Cancellation's ostensible aim is moral or ethical correction — an impulse seemingly understandable and sometimes justifiable. But as pure spectacle, public and professional humiliation quickly supersedes any project in rectitude: for many onlookers it is simply impossible to turn away.

Following cancellation, some cancelled persons may manage to glue together their shards of reputation and return in some capacity to their professions, etc. But these are the exceptions, and in most such cases this happens late, following profound psychological and geographical ostracizing, catechismal recitation of mea culpas (which tend to inspire reflexive mockery), and necessary reinvention of the cancelled person's field or their place within it.

Everyone claims to dislike the term "cancellation" yet everyone uses it anyhow. Everyone quibbles over the question of cancellation's existence as a provable societal phenomenon, which only goes to show that everyone sees there's something to it.

Cancellation mesmerizes by provoking universal dread; i.e., alert to our own foibles and errors, we all fear it. This is the point.

"Maybe a term like *social coercion* would be better,"

suggests author Jonathan Rauch, since what we call *cancellation* is often "a way for small [ideological] minorities to control conversations on a much larger scale than the quality of their ideas would normally allow them to do."

Antonyms: *complexity; debate; nuance.*

See IDEOLOGY.

("If we say we have no sin, we deceive ourselves and the truth is not in us," goes the Biblical maxim —1 John 1:8 — cited by Sir Thomas More at his own trial, a famous miscarriage of justice in 1535. More's "sinless" judges condemned him for his silence on the matter of Henry VIII's divorce, alleging that his silence indicated treason, and five days later he was beheaded. Other troubling historical analogues to current cancellation abound, such as the devastating public denunciations used commonly by the Soviet regime. Over and over, countless such denunciations delivered one preemptory message to a society of onlookers: don't let this happen to you, whoever you may be.

Having once upon a time perturbed only outspoken social media participants, our specter of cancellation now looms as a personal or professional threat in almost everyone's life.)

Clinton scandal Peccadilloes go public. Soiled dress. Impeachment.

See REALITY TV.

(I spent August 17, 1998, on a patriotic pilgrimage in

Philadelphia, visiting the sites of our nation's conception. In Independence Hall, staring at the colonial desk sets, I imagined the wigged founders' agonizing hours of debates during the momentous summer of 1776. That evening, responding to mounting public pressure, President Bill Jefferson Clinton made a live TV confession from the Oval Office, admitting to his consensual affair with Monica Lewinsky. I watched the President's remarks on a Holiday Inn television, the moral agonies of our modern republic glaringly tinged with the melodrama of miniseries. The President perched awkwardly in his chair, a condemned man spilling his guts before the primetime tribunal, doing his mighty utmost to make the whole thing seem voluntary. Was he a creep? Had he used his power for sexual advantage? Yes. And amid the mystic potency of the Jeffersonian language still ringing in my head, a jejune American present asserted itself: we hold these truths to be self-evident — I did have a relationship with Miss Lewinsky that was not appropriate...)

content (noun) That which an artist/creator is expected and almost universally encouraged to produce. Has spawned the related euphemism "content generator," referring to an individual skilled in confabulating market-optimized, highly "shareable," advertiser-alluring creative "products." Emblematic of the comprehensive downgrading of artistic endeavor to increasingly robotic, exclusively commercial ends.

See INTRAVIDUAL; MEME; TECHNOPOLY; VIRAL.

(Despite our contemporary enshrinement of "content" as a keyword of progress, popularity, and profit, what makes a work of literature lasting is its *form* as much as what it contains. The order, shape, and semi-secret palimpsest of meanings matters. The design matters. That is to say, the human art of human-made literature matters.)

context collapse An oblivious, sometimes willful, misapprehension of the complicating facts and circumstances surrounding seminal historical events or an eminent biographical case. Usually bred of cursory "research," misapplied citations, and limited education in the matter at hand. Sometimes results in "cancellations" of bygone figures.

Antonym: *education.*

See CANCELLATION (SO-CALLED); PRESENTISM.

(Alexander Pope, "An Essay on Criticism":
  "A little learning is a dangerous thing.
  Drink deep, or taste not the Pierian Spring;
  There shallow draughts intoxicate the brain,
  and drinking largely sobers us again.")

dark web A repository for the societal id. Every violence, perversion, and violent perversion is archived there: mass shooter footage, webcasted suicide footage,

footage of state-sponsored beheadings in foreign lands, brutal pornography of most varieties. Unsurprisingly — but no less shockingly — kids know how to navigate it and regularly download, memeify, and share its offerings for social currency among their peers.

Antonym: *public library*.

See INTERNET; MEME; YOUTUBE.

deep fake A virtual artifact designed to power mass manipulation, delusion, and confusion. Utilizes video editing, special effects, A.I., etc., to make a puppet of any public figure, whether in the realm of entertainment or politics, and distort their speech and/or behavior with the goal of causing them humiliation and/or subjecting them to public outrage and censure.

See MEME; PROPAGANDA; VIRAL;

dynamos Massive steam-powered electricity generators. Early colossi of a technologized, machine-driven modern world. Henry Adams, seeing a hall full of them at the Great Exposition of 1900, believed he'd seen the future. "He began to feel the forty-foot dynamos as a moral force, much as the early Christians felt the cross," writes Adams in his third-person autobiography *The Education of Henry Adams*. The dynamo was a brand of power unknown to the world till then. "Occult" in nature, it scarcely resembled the deep-rooted powers of faith that had given rise to the pagan civilizations or medieval cathedrals. "All the steam in the world could not, like the Virgin, build Chartres," Adams writes. And yet, "before the end, one began to pray to it. … Man had translated himself into a new universe which had no common scale of measurement with the old." Tomorrow had arrived, profane and overwhelming. No going back.

See MCLUHAN, MARSHALL.

Facebook, etc. Disseminate yourself as spectacle!

Antonym: *community.*

See AUGMENTED REALITY.

(I'll never forget the powerful, instantaneous endorphin flood I experienced upon first using Facebook. And how immediate, how instinctual was my mistrust of that gratification. I knew a little about the neurological basis of addiction, how the human brain will seek repetition of small, powerful pleasures, and this cast the few clear joys of Zuckerbergian social networking in a sinister light. My mind immediately pleaded, "Resist this!" while my neurological paths cried, "More!" After a month or two of struggle, I killed my profile. I've never missed it.)

filter bubble Coined by Eli Parisier in his 2011 book *The Filter Bubble: What the Internet Is Hiding from You.* A concept illustrating the fact that what one sees on a search engine, newsfeed, etc., is "filtered," thus likely different (and differently inflected politically, ideologically, aesthetically, etc.) from what someone of a different worldview will see, thanks to targeted algorithmic determinants fine-tuned to optimize user engagement (i.e., keep you always online, always scrolling) and generate maximum ad revenue (i.e., sell your attentive outrage to the highest bidder).

Synonym: *echo chamber.*

Antonym: *card catalog.*

See ALGORITHM.

Geraldo brawl November 3, 1988. Ratings skyrocket.

Antonym: *eloquence.*

See INSURRECTION; REALITY TV; RIOT.

(A white supremacist performed his imbecilic rants. An African-American man clamped his hands around the white supremacist's throat. Somebody jumped up and threw a chair. The guests, studio audience, and crew exploded in a violent mob. Next thing I knew, talk show host Geraldo Rivera's nose was a bloody mess. Yeah, they'd kept the cameras rolling. I was ten years old and I understood that what I'd seen was a big deal. Spontaneous rioting on TV was news. Soon enough, of course, it was neither news nor spontaneous. It was just TV.)

glossary Ideally an antidote to language-induced bewilderment and the epistemological obfuscations of spectacle. Ideally adaptive and flexible while also immune to the programmatic pressures of its age, and therefore worthwhile to look upon when hoping to gain perspective. Affirms by its very existence the importance of definitions, which can spare us the persuasions of convenient ideological relativism or the hammer blows of dogma.

Antonym: *harmful language list.*

See CONTEXT COLLAPSE; PRESENTISM.

(Psychiatrist and author Leslie Farber, "Lying on the Couch": "The truth that interests me is problematical, partial, modest — and still breathing. It is not normally dramatic or revelatory, and its attainment depends far more on thinking hard than feeling freely. To put it another way: I think that speaking truthfully is a more fitting ambition than speaking the truth.")

ideology A set of intellectual oversimplifications built around principles of a worldview, at first usually ambient (cultural, unconscious), rather than cherished, fervent, strident, or proselytical. In partisan politics, becomes dogma and prescriptiveness. At its extremes, rises to militancy and demands consensus, if not adherence in belief and behavior, exacerbates polarization, and may foster totalitarian dispositions and structures. Eventually inextricable from its expression through public spectacle. Defined by Lionel Trilling this way: "Ideology is not ideas; ideology is not acquired by thought but by breathing the haunted air. The life in ideology, from which none of us can wholly escape, is a strange submerged life of habit and semi-habit in which to ideas we attach strong passions but no very clear awareness of the concrete reality of their consequences."

And again, elsewhere, Trilling: "Ideology is not the

product of thought. It is the habit or the ritual of showing respect for certain formulas to which, for various reasons having to do with emotional safety, we have very strong ties and of whose meaning and consequences in actuality we have no clear understanding. ... In our culture ideas tend to deteriorate into ideology."*

Neil Postman: "[Ideological bias is] a predisposition to construct the world as one thing rather than another, to value one thing over another, to amplify one sense or skill or attitude more loudly than another."

Leon Wieseltier: "Ideology is a method for seeing less than is there. We elect to see less, in exchange for the confidence that what we have seen we have mastered. It is a satisfying contraction."

Harold Bloom: "Ideology, particularly in its shallower versions, is peculiarly destructive of the capacity to apprehend and appreciate irony. [...] Irony demands a certain attention span and the ability to sustain antithetical ideas, even when they collide with one another. [...] Irony will clear your mind of the cant of the ideologues." (In other words, ideology tends to valorize the inflexibly literal.)

Václav Havel: "Ideology is a specious way of relating to the world. It offers human beings the illusion of an identity, of dignity, and of morality while making it easier for them to part with them."

---

* From Trilling's *The Liberal Imagination*

Antonyms: *complexity; curiosity; discourse; flexibility; inquisitiveness; liberalism; thoughtfulness.*

See PROPAGANDA.

(Among the trusty indicators of intellectual, moral, and democratic health is a profound allergy to ideological oversimplification in matters of public, civic, and psychological consequence. Ideology, unchecked, inclines one to lie to oneself, and the all-but-inevitable result of having lied to oneself is that one will proceed to lie to others. But individuals and movements do not win by propounding — wittingly or not — what's untrue. Individuals and movements do not win by lying.)

insurrection (January 6th, 2021)

Antonym: *activism.*

See IDEOLOGY; INTRAVIDUAL; MEME; RIOT; VIRAL.

(Bedecked with hateful symbols, smashing and stalking their way through the corridors of the U.S. capitol and into the Senate chamber, a frothing mob set out to capture their starring roles in a cinéma vérité action movie. Would it be a hostage thriller? A shootout? The bloody birth of a new republic? Would they die onscreen? What seemed to matter most to many of them was the *footage*, the video evidence pouring into their little screens, streamed live or uploaded for a like-minded audience of "friends" and followers watching expectantly from home. What seemed to matter most was virality.)

internet Everyone's "on it." It is said that you can find anything there. Automated correlation of keywords creates, all but instantaneously, the latest "phenomenon," "happening," "news event," etc. Data breed like rabbits.

Antonym: *equanimity*.

See FACEBOOK, ETC.; MCLUHAN MARSHALL; TRENDING NOW; YOUTUBE

(We have learned to pretend — and increasingly have come to believe — that we know everything, or, what's the same, can know *anything* in a matter of minutes. We believe we choose the data, but more and more the data choose us.)

intravidual An organism already ubiquitous by the time of its christening in Dalton Conley's 2009 book *Elsewhere, U.S.A.* The *intra*vidual is determined and defined by the efficiency of this gadget or that, by lightspeed inclusion in a conversation, an argument, a realm of professed opinion chattering at *every hour* and encompassing *everywhere*. The *intra*vidual exists in a sphere of selves, a sphere that, in Mr. Conley's terms, lies perpetually elsewhere — that is, never right here right now. Through handheld screens the *intra*vidual channels work directly into their home, once a private space. Fiber optics allow the *intra*vidual to constantly import world and export self.

Antonym: *self*.

See AUGMENTED REALITY; FACEBOOK, ETC.,

IDEOLOGY; INTERNET; MCLUHAN,
MARSHALL; TECHNOPOLY.

(Today the sociological implications of the
*intra*vidual's existence are poignantly clear. Less than a
generation ago, we were subject to the laws of time as
we waited on the mail, traveled to a friend's home, or
bided the dark hours when the world's transmissions
took a pause. We were subject to ourselves: solitude
and privacy were almost unavoidable. We chose and
savored them or had them thrust upon us and learned
to make the most of them. Many of us kept journals or
diaries, recording and reflecting in sacred secrecy. If we
wished, we could clasp the covers shut with tiny locks.
Today the *intra*vidual posts his thoughts for the world
— it is not the purpose of social media to cultivate
privacy. One doesn't tuck a tweet away in a drawer and
allow its recorded contemplations to fructify in the soul.
The *intra*vidual clicks *post*, watches pixels flash into
form, and eagerly awaits comments.

We used to send messages to friends by mail,
endorsing our salutations with the slow intaglio of the
hand and creasing the papers with care. The *intra*vidual
defaults to a digital *send*, perhaps customized with
colored fonts. We used to relate voice-to-voice by
phone or face-to-face over coffee. The *intra*vidual
defaults to texts. Quickness is crucial, for the
*intra*vidual must maintain countless simultaneous
connections to other *intra*viduals elsewhere and
everywhere.

Faced with what we are becoming, it's important to recall what we have been. Dictionaries are helpful: **individual** / adj. & n. *adj. 1* single *2* particular; special; not general *3* having a distinct character *4* characteristic of a particular person *5* designed for use by one person. *n. 1* a single member of a class *2* a single human being as distinct from a family or group *3 colloq.* a person. From Middle English = indivisible.)

JFK assassination November 22, 1963. Still obsesses us. Historian Susan Jacoby notes that TV "came into its own as the chief source of breaking news" after that day. On November 24, Lee Harvey Oswald was offed on live television with a slug from Jack Ruby's revolver. On November 29, *Life* magazine published a frame-by-frame spread of images from the 8-millimter film that captured Kennedy's final, grisly moments.

See REALITY TV.

McLuhan, Marshall Misunderstood cultural interpreter of 20th- and post-20th-century America. Frequently invoked as an advocate for the electronic age, which goes to show how little the man's work is actually read. This irony is agonizing.

"Print," McLuhan writes in *The Gutenberg Galaxy* (1962), "is the technology of individualism. If men decided to modify this visual technology by an electronic technology, individualism will also be modified." Read this carefully. Try to keep the top of your head from flying off.

His four "Laws of Media" merit study by any TV viewer, Internet user, or owner of a Web-enabled device: 1) Every medium enhances something; 2) Every medium obsolesces something; 3) Every medium retrieves something from the distant past; 4) Every medium will turn on you when taken too far.

As McLuhan biographer Douglas Coupland notes, McLuhan was no sycophant of simultaneity, and what he foresaw was no technological utopia, but rather "a long painful process in which technology shifts would trigger identity collapses around the world, which would generate new and terrifying sources of disassociation between the reality of what was physically available to individuals and the unreality of a world depicted by electronic media. The result would be conflict, violence, and war."

Does our universal jones for the sleek gadget, shiny techno-bauble, and social network signify the mass mind of a consumer society in overdrive? Then McLuhan's body of thought represents the valor of enlightened nonconformity rooted in the humanities. As he writes in *The Medium is the Massage* (1967): "The poet, the artist, the sleuth — whoever sharpens our perception tends to be antisocial; rarely 'well-adjusted,' he cannot go along with currents and trends. A strange bond often exists among antisocial types in their power to see environments as they really are."

Antonym: *Mark Zuckerberg.*

See AUGMENTED REALITY; FACEBOOK, ETC.;
INTERNET; VIRAL.

meme At best a shareable joke. At worst an ersatz idea
or ideological slogan, distracting attention from real and
reasoned discourse. "Virality" is the organizing principle
and aim in the realm of meme production and
dissemination. Could be viewed as a new existential
aspiration: in lieu of becoming a person, become a meme!
 Antonyms: *discourse; idea.*
 See VIRAL.

movies Overstocked with big explosions and CGI.
Increasingly offered in 3-D or IMAX — and with
plotlines conceived to exploit these spectacular
projection technologies. Soon to be sensory-enhanced.
Viewed in Dolby-Digital-sound-equipped cinemas or
home theaters. Often deafening. Seldom ask much of the
viewer beyond fandom.
 Antonym: *cinema.*

O.J. Simpson Reporters said he was inside a white
Bronco being chased along the L.A. freeways on live
TV. Apparently he was holding a gun to his own head.
Later on, we all watched him sitting in a televised
courtroom while lawyers discussed DNA evidence, a
bloody sock, etc. In the end, he was acquitted. Roll
credits.
 See REALITY TV.

pandemic A viral phenomenon in the original epidemiological sense. Happened worldwide with Covid beginning in 2019, engendering many new controversies and heightening ideological entrenchment and polarization. Its profound repercussions include civic decay (e.g., American urban centers emptied out), social fragmentation (e.g., the widespread acceleration of screen-mediated communication), psychological detriment (e.g., conspiracy theories, paranoia, germphobia, hypochondria, etc.) and — in the case of children, teenagers, and young adults — developmental problems (social/emotional delays and educational lacunae). Its ultimate impacts will take years (maybe decades) to fully understand. Appears likely to result in a major generational divide: pre-Covid elders and post-Covid youth.

Antonym: *kiss*.

See VIRAL.

presentism Anachronistic relativism. A chronologically confused conceptual outlook invoked as the basis for many spectacular "cancellations," defenestrations, and topplings. An attempt, in some sense, to cancel time itself. A feature of context collapse, presentism asserts that positively influential but flawed persons in times past ought to have known better, behaved better, and proven themselves morally impeccable, or, as writer Kate Clanchy incisively puts it, that "the past should match an idealized present." We've deemed it permissible that any past person's chronological incapacity to exemplify the enlightened notions of our contemporary moment should discredit and disqualify them wholesale. Any or all lasting contributions this past person might have made may be rendered irrelevant or void (even if we, while acting as their inquisitors, still reap the benefits of those contributions). Signifies a wish to bowdlerize the instructively tangled story of humanity. An attitude borne, it seems, of a fundamental hubris: the refusal to recognize one's own constitutionally flawed being, insofar as every last one of us is a complex and contradictory example of the imperfectible human species existing in a particular time and in many ways unwittingly conditioned by that time.

Antonym: *complexity; maturity.*

See CANCELLATION (SO-CALLED); CONTEXT COLLAPSE.

(If I cannot take the very good despite the coexistent bad, if I do not hold tight the baby while tossing the bathwater, I may never in my life fully know another person, never sustain a mature and loving relationship, and instead labor in a cloud of lonely hypocrisy all my days. Sanctimony is not just a bad look, it's a bore.

As Alan Jacobs notes in his calm and calming book *Breaking Bread with the Dead,* the past "is other than us in a broad range of ways, and we can't control that otherness. It speaks to us in ways that we can't understand, and then (suddenly, unexpectedly) in ways we understand perfectly. [...] Access is easy; no systematic plan is required; the risks are low. But the rewards are potentially immense. [...] To confront the reality that the very same people who give us rich wisdom can also talk what seems to us absolute nonsense (and vice versa) is an education in the human condition. Including our own condition, which is likewise compounded of wisdom and nonsense."

Roosevelt Montás, *Rescuing Socrates*: "As with all thinkers from the past, our moral censure has to be applied with discrimination and historical awareness. 'In what way are they right?' is almost always a more productive and a more difficult question than 'In what way are they wrong?'"

Daveed Diggs, actor, rapper, and *Hamilton* co-star, on playing Thomas Jefferson on Broadway: "You don't have to separate these things with Jefferson: he can have written this incredible document — and several incredible documents with things that we all believe in — *and he sucks!* I think those are both true, and those have to be both true. I think we really have to stop separating them, because that's where you get into trouble. That's when you stop letting people be whole people. I disagree politically with a lot of rappers that I listen to, you know what I'm saying? There's like, sort of, rampant misogyny and homophobia in a lot of rap music. That doesn't make them less brilliant rappers — they're both true."*

---

* From the PBS documentary "Hamilton's America"

W.H. Auden, "At the Grave of Henry James":
  "Master of nuance and scruple,
  Pray for me and for all writers living or dead:
  Because there are many whose works
  Are in better taste than their lives, because there is
      no end
  To the vanity of our calling, make intercession
  For the treason of all clerks.")

Presidential debates (televised) Called "pseudo-events" by Librarian of Congress Daniel Boorstin. In September 1960, Kennedy and Nixon inaugurated the phenomenon for an audience of 70 million. This premiere of telepolitical packaging was conceived as a public service by the networks in atonement for their rigged TV quiz shows, which had been exposed the prior year. Recent televised debates have sparked chatter about "Big Bird, binders, and bayonets"; who's the "puppet"; and tax evasion as evidence of "smartness."
  Antonym: *the Lincoln Douglas debates.*
  See PSEUDO-EVENTS; REALITY TV; QUIZ SHOWS (SCANDALS).

propaganda Concerns itself solely with "answers," a pugnacious surety obtained via incessant repetition (sometimes dogmatic but more often enticingly disguised in ideological shibboleths as deep thinking or elite expertise). Aims to induce uniformity of thought and behavior. One of propaganda's antonyms is *art,* because art, real art, consists of questions and conduces to enrichment and expansion via uncertainty.

Antonyms: *art; inquiry.*

See IDEOLOGY.

protests A cherished right of the democratic citizenry in America and other modern republics. Often springing from good, clear-minded intentions, many protests are initiated in a spirit of dignity. Increasingly shown to devolve disappointingly into violence and vandalism spurred by fringe participants. This may owe at least in part to amplification and acceleration by hashtags, slogans, and ideological short-hands.

Antonym: *civil disobedience.*

See IDEOLOGY; PRESENTISM; RIOT; TWITTER.

pseudo-events Coined in Daniel Boorstin's 1961 book *The Image: A Guide to Pseudo-Events in America.* "Synthetic" happenings that are "planned, planted, or incited," which exist "primarily for the immediate purpose of being reported or reproduced," and which are interesting *because of,* rather than in spite of, their staginess. Usually dramatic, repeatable at will, cost money to create and therefore aggressively promoted, "planned for intelligibility," "planned for our convenience." Provide a "common discourse" — our knowledge of pseudo-events "becomes the test of being 'informed.'"

Antonym: *authenticity*.

See QUIZ SHOWS (SCANDALS).

quiz shows (scandals) TV scandals of the late 1950s. Game-show contestants were supplied answers ahead of time, enabling producers to maximize drama and boost sales of sponsors' products. One complicit contestant was Charles Van Doren, dashing scion of a famous intellectual family whose members boasted more than one Pulitzer Prize. Robert Redford's 1994 directorial opus *Quiz Show* recounts a version of what happened, retooled to exploit the dramatic reveals of a three-act screenplay.

Antonym: *pedagogy*.

See PSEUDO-EVENTS; REALITY TV.

(Given their uncanny resonance for our own disinformed, misinformed time of "alternative facts" and so-called "fake news," the quiz show scandals inspired my 2021 novel *Q&A*. In that book I try to get at the deeper, enduring significance of these half-forgotten events of 60 years ago: the shift of emphasis in American culture from a heritage of intellectual substance to propulsive consumer spectacle, from print values to TV values and advertising glitter, the headlong spiral into the full-color, techno-consumerist, visual media circus that characterizes us today more than ever, possibly more than anything. As we've moved from ideas to memes, from informed public discourse and debate to ideological isolation and social dissolution, from our longstanding natural analog tendencies of individual self-deception to the market-incentivized mass self-deception of our social media age with its psychotic algorithmic accelerants — *rewards come to those who fake!* — we can find not only allegorical parallels but real historical roots in those misunderstood, not-so-far-away scandals.)

reality TV Nightly national viewing. Emphatically now-based and "interactive" (*vote for your favorite contestant by text message!*). Ministers to the new demands of TV audiences: make it never-ending! Reflects the always-live simultaneity of a Web-linked world.

Antonym: *reality*.

See CLINTON SCANDAL; GERALDO BRAWL; QUIZ SHOWS (SCANDALS).

(Neverendingness in TV narratives was formerly the domain of the maligned daytime soap opera. Now that it's everywhere it's deemed respectable. Are we witnessing a deconstruction of narrative patterns, a transmutation in our understanding of what makes a story, what "good writing" is, what merits attention? Do we increasingly prefer distorted narrative structures to the "imposition" of a clear conclusion? One thing is certain: it gives advertisers more opportunity to persuade us to buy stuff.

Mass audience standards instilled by television are broadly applied as standards in other forms. For example, Nielsen ratings have staged a coup in the kingdom of literature. BookScan, originally a Nielsen product used by large bookstores and conglomerate publishers, collects point-of-sales data, which then become the main basis of editorial and inventory decisions: which books to publish, and which books to stock in stores. Whatever sells is what's read and what's read is whatever sells.)

riot Social — and often literal — conflagration; a violent disturbance involving a crowd or crowds; a paroxysm of civic incivility; a mob incitement to wreckage of property or harm of persons, powered by fanatical (if righteous) convictions and an evangelical sense of certainty; occurring among persons who find themselves, in the words of Josiah Quincy, "blown away by a torrent of passion."*

Martin Luther King, Jr., speaking at Stanford University of "The Other America," 1967: "Let me say as I've always said, and I will always continue to say, that riots are socially destructive and self-defeating. … But in the final analysis, a riot is the language of the unheard. … In a real sense our nation's summers of riots are caused by our nation's winters of delay. And as long as America postpones justice, we stand in the position of having these recurrences of violence and riots over and over again."

---

* Quincy was speaking as co-counsel to John Adams in the Boston Massacre trial of 1770.

At its purest a riot is symptomatic, a signal of ills demanding healing. And yet, as Reverend King avers, the signal itself brings further sickness. What, according to Quincy, does a mob risk making of its torrent of passion? "A shipwreck of conscience."

Antonyms: *circumspection; conscientiousness; probity; strategy.*

See IDEOLOGY.

technopoly Coined by cultural critic Neil Postman in his eponymous 1992 book. Totalitarian technocracy. The steady, erosive redefinition of history, art, truth, liberty, privacy, intelligence, communication, etc., to suit a new social order whose basis and aims are technological in nature. The use of technology for the total marginalization or imposed irrelevance of alternative or dissenting philosophies and/or whatever cannot be market optimized via technology. On par with what Václav Havel dubbed "the post-totalitarian system," i.e., a pale shade of real democracy in which the civic and moral center of a society is degraded by rampant commercialism and cynical technological materialism.

Postman: "Technopoly is a state of culture. It is also a state of mind. It consists in the deification of technology, and takes its orders from technology. This means the development of a new kind of social order. ... Those who feel most comfortable in Technopoly are those who are convinced that technical progress is humanity's supreme achievement and the instrument by which our most profound dilemmas may be solved. They also believe that information is an unmixed blessing, which through its continued and uncontrolled production and dissemination offers increased freedom, creativity, and peace of mind. The fact that information does none of these things — but quite the opposite — seems to change few opinions, for such unwavering beliefs are an inevitable product of the structure of Technopoly. In particular, Technopoly flourishes when the defenses against information break down."

Antonym: *civic life.*

See A.I.; AUGMENTED REALITY.

trending now A sidebar that once designated up-to-the-minute topics of online interest. An Internet mirror. We've moved in these latter years toward the totality of the "hashtag" as an indexer of societal fixations, but are we any less omnivorous in our distraction than we're shown to be in the following snapshot from three days after our 2012 Presidential election? "1) Facebook Obama slur; 2) Dana White superfight; 3) *World War Z*; 4) Lindsay Lohan cancels; 5) Waffle House; 6) Alexa Vega; 7) Black Friday 2012; 8) Groupon; 9) Breast cancer; 10) 2016 election."—Yahoo.com, Nov. 9, 2012, 10:40 p.m."

Antonym: *the classics.*

See FILTER BUBBLE; INTERNET.

(I need only imagine reading an alternative inventory

of trending searches and I am re-sensitized to the squandered potential of our technologized lives:
1. Eradicating poverty; 2. Teacher pay raises;
3. Universal free healthcare as a human right; 4. Nation-wide transportation infrastructure investments; 5. Agri-business regulation; 6. Growing the middle class; 7. Arts & Humanities funding; 8. Deprivatizing political campaign funding; 9. Reduction of carbon emissions; 10. Great works of literature.)

twitter An Internet popularity contest waged via cursory dispatches from members of respective ideological bubbles. Propelled by and propels social polarization. Feeds on metrics and encourages its "users" to do the same. Perhaps most effective among online platforms in making the collection of a blob-like mass of "followers" a primary aspiration for much of the digital citizenry.
   Antonym: *birdsong*.
   See FACEBOOK; INTRAVIDUAL; VIRAL.

video games Immersive and virtual-reality-oriented nowadays. Mesmerizing: some have died at the console, neglecting to interrupt play to attend to basic bodily needs. Grown-ups play them — and admit to doing so.
   Antonym: *live theater*.
   See AUGMENTED REALITY

viral Considered by many, for a long time and in most

situations, an undesirable qualifier. Popularized at the dawn of our millennium by Malcolm Gladwell in his book *The Tipping Point* (itself a "viral" bestselling publishing sensation). Gladwell's book helped spark a cultural flash of non-connotative thinking, as the once-worrisome epidemiological term was rebranded by hip TED-talkers, slick marketeers, and self-congratulatory digerati. Thereafter considered by many the description of a desired outcome; i.e., a rapid rise to popularity and a vast sociological endorsement sure to spawn a book deal, an enviable job offer, media invites, social and industry cache, and various lucrative contractual agreements.

Antonyms: *healthy; honorably obscure; underrated; unsung; well-kept secret.*

See ADAPTATION; BINGE; MEME.

(The fun lasted until precisely the moment on March 11, 2020 when the World Health Organization restored definitively to living awareness the original precise meaning of "viral.")

window A thing one stares through, which functions as a portal to a real and palpable world beyond our immediate bodily space. In the newer usage "window" increasingly refers to a facsimile on a digitized screen: a thing we stare *at.* In this customizable virtual form (its parameters neatly subject to our preferences and controls) a window, by its design, curtails broader perspective or immediate immersion in a physically accessible space beyond our command.

Antonym: *pixels.*

See AUGMENTED REALITY; FILTER BUBBLE.

YouTube "Broadcast Yourself" is the motto. "See what the world is watching" is the motto. "Punch that SUBSCRIBE button" and "Smash that LIKE button" are the desperate exhortations of all YouTube "content creators." Google owns it, bottomlessly absorbing your data and applying omnipotent algorithms as you watch, in order to serve up your next recommendation through the supercharged delivery mechanism of autoplay.

Antonym: *reading.*

See BINGE; INTERNET.

(My son tells me about this YouTube video where a cat licks an outlet and the lights go out with a concussive crack; about this YouTube video where a middle-aged guy inexplicably falls and strikes his forehead on the floor and says "e-no"; about this YouTube video where Donald Duck masturbates; about this YouTube video where a mom and dad mock their adolescent son for the camera; about this YouTube video where a guy reviews key components common to most school shootings; about this YouTube video where middle-aged men spot bloodthirsty clowns peering in through the living room window; about this YouTube video where young men perform handstands on the edge of skyscraper roofs; about this YouTube video...)

Zenith My first TV set, ten-inch screen, black-and-white, rabbit ears, knobs for changing channels. How many hours did I pour into that little box? Glorious passivity, gorgeous illusion. How I loved it!

Antonym: *nadir.*

Why We Need the Humanities, a Fragment of a Talk *

The confidence of the artist and the humanist
generally has not been at one of its historical
peaks during our own period. We have become
very defensive and to that extent participate in
the rigidities of defense.
  —W. Jackson Bate, *The Burden of the Past and
  the English Poet*

1.

Humans Teaching Humans

I MMEDIATELY WE MAY NOTICE the way our title,
"Why We Need the Humanities," invites
assertions and defenses. Many of us are familiar
with one particular defense along these lines, designed
to protect Humanities departments at colleges and
universities. Sometimes, too, it's invoked as a defense of
Humanities curricula in public schools. We might call
this the Institutional Defense. Dignified and business-
like in style, expert-driven in substance, the
Institutional Defense revolves around compelling data
points, convincing statistical results, surveys and polls,

---

*Adapted from a talk presented to the faculty of the University
of California Berkeley's Academic Talent Development
Program.

and careful sociological studies. You can be sure you're hearing the Institutional Defense whenever someone cites test scores to demonstrate cognitive gains in students who engage with Humanities curricula, or when someone makes a case for why the Humanities are economically relevant — that is, how "Humanities skills" apply in the job market, how respected employers hunger for these skills in prospective employees. The Institutional Defense often centers on the keyword *innovation*. That is, it's a defense tailor-made to demonstrate how a solid Humanities education inculcates critical thinking skills, creative problem solving, out-of-the-box idea generation — all of which fuel the *innovation* that's the engine of our future economy. Etc., etc., etc.

If nothing else, the Institutional Defense is a starting point. We could look, for example, at compelling data from a case study in the field of public education: Willow Elementary in Napa, California — a neighborhood school not long ago designated as "failing." In its first year implementing school-wide Humanities-infused curricula, Willow Elementary set an overall growth target of five points on state achievement tests. At the close of that year, when the tests reflected a "24-point gain overall," the State of California smelled an error. The tests were reevaluated, and indeed, an error was discovered. In fact, the gain at Willow Elementary was not 24 points but 28!

We lean into the data, we consider sub-groups of students, we note how the gains shook out among them:

- o Hispanic students: expected growth: 6 pts
     / actual: 25
- o White students: expected growth: 0 pts
     / actual: 31
- o Economically disadvantaged students:
     expected growth: 6 pts / actual: 33
- o ESL students: expected growth: 7 pts
     / actual: 24 *

The Institutional Defense cherishes this stuff. And what's not to love?

In the professional realm, it turns out to be relatively simple matter to prove employer demand for the "skills" a Humanities education fosters. Exactly how does the profile of the ideal future employee match the profile of a Humanities major? We need only turn to big-shot business guy David Rubenstein, co-founder of the global investment firm The Carlyle Group. The *New York Times* quoted Rubenstein making a passionate case for the value of a Humanities education. "Many of Wall Street's top executives studied the Humanities," said Rubinstein. "The reasoning skills that

---

* Source: "How Did You Learn Today? The Artful Learning Case Study," video, YouTube
https://www.youtube.com/watch?v=v7VMV_jh7g0 (accessed 26 February, 2023)

come with a well-rounded Humanities education actually result in higher-paying jobs over time." And he went on to coin his own formula for success in the field: "H = MC. Humanities equals more cash."**

The Institutional Defense is valuable. The Institutional Defense is convincing. The Institutional Defense is important. But as I take up the invitation to make assertions and defenses, my own focus moves elsewhere. I'm a teacher and creative worker engaged in the lifelong project of education, and it's from this perspective that I wish to proceed. So in considering why we need the Humanities I'd like to step away from the stuff of well-intentioned TED talks and insider op-eds. Instead, I'd like to consider something fairly unquantifiable, something hard to demonstrate in data — something along the lines of what the twentieth-century art critic Herbert Read meant when he remarked:

> Only insofar as a society is rendered sensitive by the arts (and Humanities) do ideas become accessible to it.

The parenthetical there is mine. I've nudged the Humanities into Read's phrasing — I don't think he'd object. Read's statement, given our thoughtful reflection, seems only to increase in its rightness. Read

---

** Source: https://dealbook.nytimes.com/2014/01/23/carlyle-co-founders-formula-for-success-study-the-humanities

is saying we can't learn much — and it follows that we can't make much progress as a society — unless we first activate a certain *human sensitivity*. This clear and simple notion — that the arts and Humanities are an indispensable foundation for everything else we hope to learn, know, and achieve — lies at the heart of my own decidedly less institutional (and more pedagogical) argument. So let me try some variations on our guiding imperative. We could phrase it this way: Why Teachers Need the Humanities *in Their Teaching*.

Or, to refine the matter further: *Why Teachers Need the Humanities in Their Teaching as Humans Teaching Other Humans.*

Or, in search of still greater precision, how about this: *Why a Humanities-infused Style of Inquiry Makes Sense, as Teachers Think About Their Own Teaching Practices as Humans in a Human Classroom Space with Human Students.*

———

So MUCH TALK ABOUT *HUMANS* and *humanity* immediately sends my mind to the following images. In a word or two, what do these images show us? What do we see?

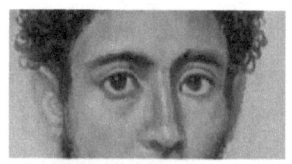

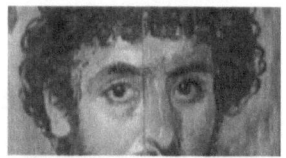

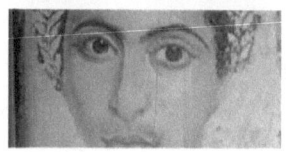

Human eyes. Eyes looking out — and that they are looking out *at us* we have no doubt. These are remarkably penetrating — even haunting — gazes. Vividly, these eyes tell us something about these people — but what, exactly? Giving them our long consideration, what can we say these eyes communicate? Certainly there's poignancy here, but of what kind? Is it a poignant longing? Sorrow? Regretful curiosity? Any of these — all of these — seem reasonable emotional responses to these indelible looks.

Next, we might ask: Across what measure of distance do these eyes gaze in order to see us? And perhaps because the communicative effect here is itself so immediate, we feel confident in answering this question without hesitation. The distance is short. These eyes feel *close*. Intimate, even.

Last question: How recently were these images created? Nineteenth century? Earlier? The Renaissance? Earlier still? Perhaps the Middle Ages.

In fact, these eyes originate in a tradition of painting known as Fayum Portraiture, from Roman Egypt, in the first century A.D. They were painted from life and intended to serve as funeral portraits. After the sitter's death, the portrait would adorn the head of that person's mummy.

So much for basic historical context. Now let's step back again, still looking, and ask one more time: *What do we see here?*

Still, of course, the answer is that we see human eyes. Deeply human eyes, yes, but that's merely a noun. In fact we're also seeing a verb. Something is *happening* with these astonishing images, or happening through them, and in our initial descriptive attempts, we have already grazed what this is. The phrase "human eyes," heard aloud, verbalizes the paintings' most profound action and effect: *Humanize.*

These human eyes — no less expressive despite their removal in time, not at all remote despite the lapse of two millennia — make an unmistakable *humanizing* impact.

———

W HAT DOES IT MEAN TO HUMANIZE an idea or a person? The power of the Fayum gazes, so affectingly reaching across time and space, offers a suggestion. The Fayum Portraits embody History. They embody Culture. They're Art and, as the residue of an ancient belief system, they're also Philosophy. They are, then, emblematic of the Humanities.

What they exemplify precisely is a vital and enlivening trans-chronological power, an overcoming of strangeness, unfamiliarity, and cultural difference (in this case the gap between bygone Roman Egypt and us, now, wherever on earth these images may find us). This enlivening is the humanizing impact of the Humanities — the capacity to sensitize students to the vivid reach of time, and to the manifold nature of time generally.

In a 1998 essay responding to the Fayum Portraits, John Berger captures these exemplary qualities:

> The future has been, for the moment, downsized, and the past is being made redundant. Meanwhile, the media surround people with an unprecedented number of images, many of which are faces. The faces harangue ceaselessly by provoking envy, new appetites, ambition or, occasionally, pity combined with a sense of impotence. Further, the images of all these faces are processed and selected in order to

harangue as noisily as possible, so that one appeal out-pleads and eliminates the next appeal. And people come to depend upon this impersonal noise as a proof of being alive! Imagine then what happens when somebody comes upon the silence of the Fayum faces and stops short. Images of men and women making no appeal whatsoever, asking for nothing, yet declaring themselves, and anybody who is looking at them, alive! They incarnate, frail as they are, a forgotten self-respect. They confirm, despite everything, that life was and is a gift.*

To humanize a person or an idea involves discovering — through imagination, creativity, and human inquiry — a direct connection that enlivens person or idea despite time and distance. There's a uniquely communalizing aspect to this capacity for reaching and enlivening, which bears visceral relevance in a time like ours: a time recently marred and divided by a global pandemic.

It's remarkable to recall the many things that served, amid enforced isolation, to communalize us during Covid-19. And we can reflect on how each of these things illustrated, in its own way, the richly human power of *reaching across.* Always imagination and creativity played a primary role. Take, as just one

---

* From Berger's *The Shape of a Pocket*

example, The Swan Project, an online video produced during early lockdowns, presenting 24 musicians across 12 countries in an unbroken relay performance of Saint-Saëns's cello piece "The Swan." Immediately evident here is the enlivening transgression of geographical space. But The Swan Project is just as much a reach across time. Composed by Saint-Saëns in 1889, the simple melody of "The Swan" resonates with immediate emotional power in our contemporary global circumstances.*

2.

Imagination Training

> The task of the teacher as instructor is to introduce the pupil to facts which have no immediate practical significance. (If there were no such facts, or if they composed an unimportant part of our inheritance, a teacher would be a luxury rather than a necessity.)
> —Michael Oakeshott, "Learning and Teaching"

HAVING CONSIDERED the uniquely communicative capacity of the Humanities — what they're capable of *doing* — let's step back to clarify what they *are*. The Humanities

---

* The Swan Project is freely available as a video online

encompass various specializations and areas of scholarship, but specialization is not their ultimate aim. When I say "the Humanities" throughout this discussion my meaning is particular, not necessarily conventional, and decidedly not academic.

We can understand the Humanities as a wide-open style of inquiry that is *experiential* in nature and encompasses Literature, History, Philosophy, and Art. The Humanities seek connections between these subject areas and countless other fields of inquiry. In simplest terms, the Humanities are history and culture. And as history and culture they are inherently and essentially interdisciplinary.

Having asserted that the Humanities reach not only across time and space, but across disciplines (which we'll explore further in a moment), I'd like to emphasize that their effects are, fundamentally, *experiential*. It's a rich experience to sense the humanizing power of the Fayum Portraits or Saint-Saëns's "The Swan" coming across to us undiminished despite time and space. The effects are communalizing as well. All of which is to say, the Humanities establish and emphasize a communal human experience. Just how they do so is my focus now, and as we proceed toward an answer we require just one word: imagination.

If we think about what is most essentially human, one capacity above any other that truly characterizes us *as humans*, this is what we come to: the Imagination. The Humanities express a great deal about the human condition, and at their most powerful they serve to educate us through *imagination training.*

Imagination training is education grounded in the human experience — in questions that we cannot avoid and that we will not escape. Imagination training is education grounded in the universal predicament of finding ourselves plunked down alive without instructions, aware of having emerged from nonexistence, and aware, also, of our eventual return to nonexistence. The human experience is the experience of being a meaning-seeking creature, of nurturing a creative mind, and possessing a moral conscience. As I see it, this grounding in the human experience should be foremost on the mind of any teacher, no matter their subject. The finest teachers — whatever their subject may be — will ask themselves constantly: *in what ways is my teaching speaking to human beings? In what ways is my teaching speaking to my students' essential human questions?*

James Baldwin, one of our great American writers, speaks to the essential need for this grounding, this imagination training, in his blazingly insightful 1959 essay "The Discovery of What It Means to Be an American." Baldwin writes:

> Though we do not wholly believe it yet, the interior life is a real life, and the intangible dreams of people have a tangible effect on the world.

Here Baldwin makes a fundamental assertion about human imagination. The interior life is a real life. Broadly speaking, can we be said to believe this yet?

Baldwin was writing as an American expatriate, having gone to France to escape the racial strife of his segregated homeland. In avouching the reality of the interior life, he was speaking as a black man, a gay man, and a creative writer. He faced, in the mid-twentieth-century United States, ostracization on three fronts: his skin color, his sexual orientation, and his imagination. On the bases of skin color and sexual orientation Baldwin was subject to legally codified discrimination. And he was no less subject to deleterious forces on the basis of his imagination. In that latter domain the forces working against him included social repression (of his ideas and creative expressions), state intimidation (he was extensively surveilled by the FBI), economic invalidation (writers struggle mightily in America), and relentless practical and spiritual discouragement. As in much of Baldwin's writing, the wonder of his words here lies in their decisiveness, their prophetic truth-telling about a fundamental human quality: interiority.

Baldwin's terms can spawn a series of reflective questions for anyone who teaches:

o Are we awake, sensitive, and intent on nurturing the interior life in our students?
o How does the interior life relate to

mathematics, or to science, or to social
studies?
- o How might one better honor the student's
  interior life through the style in which one
  transmits a subject?
- o How does one draw out the relationship, for
  the student, between the subject and their
  interior life as a creative, imaginative,
  meaning-seeking human?

By responding mindfully to these questions, a teacher
can begin to foster the special kind of open-ended
imagination training for which the Humanities are
uniquely optimal.

While keeping Baldwin's words in mind, I'd like to
turn to another great creative thinker of the twentieth
century, Virginia Woolf, who writes:

> There must be two levels of being: the surface
> and the spreading depths. To tell the whole
> story of a life a writer must devise a means by
> which the two levels of existence could be
> recorded.

Here, in Woolf's phrase *the surface and the spreading
depths*, I find something analogous to Baldwin's
assertion about the "interior life." Woolf is musing
about the effects she wants to achieve in her novelistic
writing. But it occurs to me that we could fiddle
slightly with her wording and arrive at an astonishing

reflection about teaching and what we seek to achieve as teachers. That would look like this:

> There must be two levels of *teaching*. To tell the whole story of a *subject* a *teacher* must devise a means by which the two levels, *fact (i.e., surface) and experience (i.e., depths)* could be *explored...*

It is this we think about when we think about how the Humanities offer an indispensable imagination training: a kind of teaching that provides the subject *and* a *humanizing experience* of the subject.

2.5

Narrative Questions

BEFORE WE GO ON, I'd like to describe how I came to teaching.

Like many teachers, I arrived through a side-door. In my case the side-door was the creative, artistic life. This was nearly twenty years ago and my first novel had just been published. Here I am back then, on the rear flap of that book jacket, trying my best to stare holes into the literary critics before they descend. I was almost as serious as this photo makes me look. For the person pictured here, writing was everything —

novel writing in particular.

An unusual way of using the mind, writing a novel is a special experience, requiring a great deal of patience in the face of unknowns, uncertainty, and ambiguity. It also requires a great deal of discipline: as it can be surprisingly tedious, novel writing demands a special commitment to the intricacies of process. Moreover, a novel almost always asks its writer to face their own ignorance on any number of subjects. These can include historical events, geographical settings, vocational details, special lexicons, and identities unlike the writer's own identity. The novelist's work involves facing, with painful frankness, how little they know, and then doggedly setting out to acquire the missing knowledge. Given the imaginative context of the novelist's work, however, the key to the novelist's learning process is that they must *come up with the right questions.* Imaginative questions, novelistic questions —

these constantly carry the novelist outside of their comfort zones, which means moving into subject areas where, at first, the novelist has no rightful expertise.

A novel demands that its writer commit to this weird and foggy process of imaginative inquiry and allow the time required to make the book well. This is often, at a minimum, years. During these years, the novelist must understand and accept a difficult truth: that they may end up with nothing to show for all their work. In most cases, the novelist labors without guarantee that anybody will ultimately publish their novel. Nevertheless, they are charged to continue working, to embrace the many unknowns that come with continuing, and to find some assurance in "the long view."

I've spent the last 25 years in this experience, laboring away on one novel after another, publishing one every four or five years. Meanwhile, amid this writing life steeped in the imagination and the circuitous creative process, I've found myself undertaking more and more teaching work. The more I've taught, the more I've come to recognize affinities between the novel-writing process and the teaching life. That is, the questions that drive my process as a novelist are often exactly the questions I can apply in my teaching, as I think about how to best communicate with my students. They are questions of narrative:

o How do I structure and plot this?

- o What's the form?
- o Who are the main characters?
- o What do I want the students to ask?
- o What are the themes?
- o How is meaning achieved?
- o How can I defamiliarize this? (resensitize myself and the reader or student)
- o How will I communalize this?
- o How do I make this relevant?

Narrative questions are teaching questions.

3.

Exploration & Synthesis

INQUIRY, IMAGINATION TRAINING, Narrative Questions — these things bring us to the concept of synthesis.
Here's a stanza from Ralph Waldo Emerson:

I thought the sparrow's note from heaven,
Singing at dawn on the alder bough;
I brought him home, in his nest, at even;
He sings the song, but it cheers not now,
For I did not bring home the river and sky;—
He sang to my ear, — they sang to my eye.

Emerson's poetic analogy here points to the

important fact that delight, the enlivening sensation, is achieved through different elements working together. This is a poem about context, the bigger picture, integrated experience, the holistic, the surface and the spreading depths — what we can call synthesis. It's synthesis of this kind toward which we're constantly guiding our students. What exactly does synthesis mean for students? It means they get to experience the bird in its natural setting. It means bird and birdsong *and* river *and* sky — a more complete picture. It means that their learning is connected to a larger experience.

Emerson said it in prose too, in his mystical essay "Circles":

> Each new step we take in thought reconciles twenty seemingly discordant facts.

———

T HESE ARE SIGNAL WORDS: synthesis and experience. And they bring to mind a cognitive issue that child development psychologist Alison Gopnik describes when she outlines something she calls the "Explore-Exploit tension." Here's what Gopnik says:

> You've got one creature that's really designed to explore, to learn, to change. That's the child. And then you've got this other creature

that's really designed to exploit, as computer scientists say, to go out, find resources, make plans, make things happen. ... Adults have the capacity, to some extent, to go back and forth between those two states. But I think that babies and young children are in that explore state all the time. That's really what they're designed to do.*

Psychology research like that which Gopnik undertakes in her post at the University of California Berkeley tells us that babies and young children are masterful explorers. In contrast to the explorative mindset of these very young people, adults are much more accustomed to an exploit mindset. Explore versus Exploit: because we've all been children ourselves, we're already intuitively familiar with this counterpoint. And as educators we can connect this idea to how we think about the learning process, the absorption of new knowledge, the formation of new understanding in a classroom space. To boil it down to an essence, we might even say that there are two ways of looking at education and the aims of education. On one side, we have an emphasis on verbs like these:

SYNTHESIZE / EXPLORE / EXPERIENCE

And on the other side, we emphasize verbs like these:

---

* The Ezra Klein Show (podcast), April 2021

SPECIALIZE / EXPLOIT / EXTRACT

And maybe these verb groups aren't always in strict opposition — maybe they exist in relationship on a spectrum. Maybe there are gradations. Maybe sometimes we move from synthesis toward specialization and back, and so on. But we could take these two ways of looking at education and conceptualize each one as a motivating question. First, a question that's immediately familiar:

What will you do with your education?

At some point in our lives we have this question posed to us, in so many words, perhaps during a holiday gathering or a family reunion. A clear reflection of one of those two ways of looking at education, this question falls, of course, on the side of specializing, extracting, exploiting. It is a question rooted in a utilitarian view of education, insofar as the question relates directly to economic anxieties, the job market, and matters of social status.

On the other side would be a very different motivating question, reflecting a broader way of thinking about education and its aims:

What will your education do *with you?*

This is the *Humanities-oriented question,* or the

question that a Humanities-infused education encourages us to ask. Falling on the side of synthesizing, exploring, and experiencing, it is simultaneously a question couched in larger questions about life, existential realities, and emotional wellbeing. Centered in the human condition, it opens to moral and philosophical dimensions.

So we may, as good "extractive" adults, cultivate and propound *a fixed idea* about education and its aims: specialization, exploitation, money, career, status. Or we may, as adults who were also children once, adults who recognize and retain something of our original dynamic capacity as creatures "designed to change," cultivate and propagate a broader idea of education as potentially *transformative* — that is, as an open-ended explorative process, an accrual of synthesized experiences leading to transformation that we can't necessarily foresee...*

---

* The talk continued with an object lesson focused on a single sonnet by William Shakespeare and designed to illustrate the kind of humanizing inquiry, imagination training, and synthesis that Shakespeare's sonnet can occasion as it reaches us across time. Too sprawling to include in these pages, among the surprising panoply of things that this inquiry touched on were: astronomy and navigational science; cultural attitudes about romantic love; the musical and literary concept of counterpoint and the physiological basis of rhythm; mythological symbolism from ancient Greece to the 19th century; exponential numbers, the biology of the cicada; the music of Bach; and 20th-century African American experience in the urban northeast.

Variations on Questions Posed to Young Writers During Lockdown (2020)

How PARTICULAR is the seeing your mind accomplishes?

Can you look at things so intensely they seem to look back?

What will they say then?

  (*You*, Rilke heard, *must change your life*)

Can you re-sensitize your perceptions, attuned to new rhythms?

Can you bear in mind: imagination starts at the window?

  (and sometimes one finds the window is dream)

  (and dream — like rhythm, and like clarity — is achieved, not granted)

Can you begin, and proceed, in the awareness that your characters, those persons of paper and whim, know more than you can know now?

Know more, perhaps, than you or I will ever know?

And can you bear in mind, too, that their chief attribute — their relationship to time — makes them and you so very much alike?

> (and them and I)

> (and you and I)

Can you bear in mind: to write the name of a person or place means committing to an exploration of time's effects on that person and in that place?

An exploration of the secrets your people carry — their hopes, their ghosts, and regrets?

> (even as these people shelve and layer, in the moving frame of their disguised skeletons, contradictions uniquely their own)

Can you bear in mind: we are each of us more than just one thing?

Can you bear in mind: this one life passing in counterpoint to all?

This one moment in counterpoint to all?

How it amounts to more than one thing?

What rhythms arrive as time flows and pools, as time turns to body and sense?

What rhythms arrive in the limbic motion of each line and the lingual expression leaping white space on a page?

What rhythms?

What sounds abound bundling and tumbling in bounty past confines of mind?

Once uncoupling, once unshackling habit from impression, can you find yourself lifted upon sudden words to meet the glimmer and flow of sight?

To find the world ever new, new even in its ancientness?

Will you recognize and bear in mind: the work at hand consists of this alertness? (nothing less)

Notice and bear in mind: how wondrously stocked are these noiseless sheltering spaces, our rooms?

What utterance awaits patiently in the many unheeded objects?

Are your ears refreshed?

Are you attuned anew?

Are you listening, quarantined alive?

Will you bear in mind the thing the young writers, alive, reminded me?

("Time," they said, "belongs to no one in particular")

Variations on a Rough Draft

I N THE BACKYARD AS A BOY, whether spying on the neighbors, throwing lemons in their pool, tormenting our schnauzer on his lead, scrutinizing the anatomy of the buzzing pollinators in the lemon tree (their transparent silver-threaded wings pinched between finger and thumb)   whether prying up the hatch in the backyard decking, the door to the crawlspace, and shimmying down along the dry cool earth beneath our floorboards, on my back and listening to my mother's movements in the rooms above, her every step a consequence, a vibration in the very structure of things   whether donning a Zorro mask to play burglar and with pillowcase in hand creeping down the block and into the Loshki family's house in search of the son's coveted marble collection (what did I bring home? and did we all leave our house-doors unlocked? such nonchalant expectations about the order and welcome of things?)   whether as the younger brother discovering the pornographic magazine thrown aside in the storm drain at the end of our block, its pages warty and water-curled and half bleached away, and bringing back the report of this alien inheritance to brother and friend, and dividing the images amongst ourselves — my brother, Sal Loshki, and me, and claiming for keeps the tattered scrap of a woman's green eye — and bringing it back to secret away under a shingle in my bedroom wall, forever after aware of the wall as my watcher — eye of God, eye of life, of the future, of the mute faraway unknown and still undreamt future   whether protected, whether endangered, whether vulnerable, whether ignorant, whether aware of the earthquakes always held in abeyance along the forked and weedy imbrications of the nearby San Andreas, the nearby Loma Prieta, the earth itself our Shiva   whether at the epicenter, whether on the outskirts, whether self-perceiving, whether self-deluded, but granted a beginning, a center and all its impossible radii — what was there, what was there *ever*, except impression?

———

T HE DEEP BREATH THE STRINGS PLAYER TAKES before the first vibration of the bow — heard in the audible secrecy of tape recordings. Inspire: the mind and body's music. Respire: the sound itself, the motions that make it heard. Inspire: brain waves, memory waves, the artist's intention. Respire: sound waves, vibratory expression, intention reincarnate.

———

T HE EVENING SENSATIONS. That is, when evening was enough to bring on sensations all its own. Something in the new radiance of lights, some quality in the air, some matter of temperature. The pressure letting off. The reprieve, the exhale, the loosening of one's walk, the soft and heightened *clarity* of everything one saw.   Riding in the backseat of the family station wagon, my father driving, my siblings and our parents all together in the blue crushed suede of the interior, heading home from Sunday evening church service, the dusk languorous, rich in its crystalline depths. The traffic signals looked newly polished in their colors, the stripes in the asphalt newly white, the storefronts just closing, the signs and mannequins suddenly, at daylight's end, retrospectively dignified.

It took the dark forever to do its job, and we saw no cause to fear its arrival. The evening had brought it, after all, leading it home with us like a woman on its arm, letting her go ahead at the door. Back at our house, still acute and aglow, we felt our way through the blackness of the room to the switch on the wall, where the euphoria ended with a flick — until the next time, and for as long as it could last in the years of evenings ahead.

———

WHAT EVERY HUMAN PASSES ON, what is handed like an old bearskin down the generations, is the consciousness of time. Teach — because you were taught — to denominate, divvy up, and fractionize the hours. Bells ring, doors shut, gifts are given, hugs and kisses, flowers, money, heirlooms. One learns to say hello and goodbye. One has one's piñatas, white dresses, first car crash. Blinds go up, blinds go down, the furniture is sheeted in August and the following June the dust astonishes. Comment on the height and flow of the creek. Feed and water one's body. Receive guests and learn to accept hospitalities. Tolerate the indiscretions of medical exams, of medicines. Learn things, forget them, and later try to remember ever knowing them at all. Marvel at the ingenuity of children, the vividness of children, of childhood concerns. Remember school's boredom and its extravagant excitements. Read and sleep and stare into space. Remember the chimney needs cleaning, car needs servicing, foundation needs patching, garage needs sweeping, and find the time. Always, eventually, one finds the time though time is immense and one's own share so meager and so easily misplaced in that immensity. One finds the time, and one has long since taken this to heart: the days are always shrinking and one is busy parceling out the hours, using up the days. One finds the time. Or does not — but time continues. We are good heirs, and good benefactors.

—

W HEN WE ARE YOUNG we are largely insane.
"There is a great swelling inside me, like a good
current, now that I've arrived, now that it's quiet, now
that I've settled to work." A note in a young man's
journal. He writes it during his first week alone in
Lowell, Massachusetts, where he has moved, sight
unseen, into a twelve-by-twelve room in which he
intends to become a writer. He's twenty years old. "K
said the other night on the phone, 'All this has been
brewing for so long!' Yes. The waters were churned.
Now they'll begin to break." The metaphors transfixed
him, their mixing didn't concern him.

The young man's arrival in Lowell had followed an
eight-day train journey from California. He lugged a
large rucksack jam-packed with all his clothing, having
shipped ahead in a single carton the rest of his
belongings. Inside the carton: one deflated air mattress,
two lightweight blankets (rolled), one small table lamp,
one frying pan, one pot, two plates, two cups, forks
knives spoons (two of each), one bath towel, one hand
towel, a packet of small pictures and postcards, a small
container full of books, a ream of white printer paper. In
a separate box, painstakingly wrapped in parcel paper,
he'd shipped a brand new Brother Selectric word
processor.

"An honest man has hardly need to count more than

his ten fingers," went the words of Thoreau, in one of those innumerable passages from *Walden* that resounded daily in the young man's head. "Or in extreme cases he may add his ten toes, and lump the rest. Simplicity, simplicity, simplicity!" It was *Walden* and the spirit of Thoreau that had led the young man to Massachusetts.

From the Lowell station he set off walking for 1861 Middlesex Street, his new address. The heat was oppressive on that late-August day, and the town was a gloomy shock of brick factory buildings, all abandoned. Strewn trash, boarded houses, derelict storefronts, downtrodden figures. Sirens wailed. Cars sputtered. A cab driver sprayed spittle when asked the fare to Concord. "Concord! Wha' the fuck ya wanna go to Concord fa, buy herbal spices?"

This place was as near to Concord as the young man could afford, fourteen miles as the crow flies, but how bizarre the difference that short distance could make. Here he was in the cradle — not of American Romantic genius, but of a moribund industrial revolution. In lieu of the inspirations and pastoral idylls of old Concord, Lowell provided the desecrations of mass-produced waste. And it just so happened to be the birthplace of Jack Kerouac, a drug-addled fun-house Thoreau.

The young man kept walking and tuned his brain to the counsel of *Walden*. "I know of no more encouraging fact than the unquestionable ability of man to elevate his life by a conscious endeavor. ... To affect the quality of the day, that is the highest of arts. ... Follow your genius closely enough, and it will not fail to show you a fresh prospect every hour."

The young man had it in mind that a task of immense importance lay before him. He'd believed he was coming to Massachusetts in order to realize a Renaissance fantasy. Neighbor to the vivid ghosts of Romantic America — Thoreau, Emerson, Alcott, Hawthorne — he would help lay the foundation of a literary rebirth.

When we are young we're largely insane, but it is because it's our primary business at that time to be lost in our own minds. (Later on we become lost in time.)

———

"IF ONE LISTENS to the faintest but constant suggestions of his genius, which are certainly true, he sees not to what extremes, or even insanity, it may lead him; and yet that way, as he grows more resolute and faithful, his road lies." —Thoreau

———

(Include here excerpts from letter(s) written in Lowell, in that increasingly cold and dark autumn when the young man is twenty and living immaculately alone in a shabby twelve-by-twelve room with an air mattress, a plastic lawn chair, a small row of books, and a word processor, as he passes weeks upon weeks reading and writing and, if the frigid weather permits, taking walks, and never speaking to anyone.)

————

THE MORNING THE YOUNG MAN was to leave California, he woke in his parents' house at 4:00 AM to sit with his father in the living room. The father and mother had long since accepted the young man's fierce, all-consuming belief in his "mission." For weeks they'd watched him fervently preparing and never so much as questioned the wisdom of his scheme.

Now in the dead of the dark early morning the father shared his faith in the young man, told the young man how much he believed in what he was doing. Then, moved to tears, he imparted to his son the secret of his own life's fulfillment. After that they embraced. The young man watched his father step out the front door, leaving for work at 4:15 AM on this day like every other, without despair.

————

D AY AFTER DAY IN MASSACHUSETTS the young
man sat in self-confinement putting down words,
reading, putting down further words. All the time he
was asking himself, What is a voice? What is a style?
What do I mean to say? How will I manage to say it?
How, in my saying of it, will I banish untruth from the
expression?

———

M ARCEL PROUST: "Style is the transformation the
writer imposes on reality."

———

T HE NARROW STAIRWELL smells of curry and
cabbage as the young man climbs to his room. He hears
the neighbors but rarely sees them. In a ground-floor
apartment every evening a family performs prayers,
ringing small bells for a quarter of an hour. In the
young man's kitchenette there's a mild odor of gas. One
of the stove burners won't light. In the room's exterior
wall there's a chink at one corner of the swamp heater
— crouching, he sees daylight through it. At night a
draft whistles there. His door is battered. When closed
it hangs askew in its frame. There is a single lock: a

deadbolt at shoulder-height. There is a peephole. And there is an intercom and buzzer through which, by accident one night, he unlocks the downstairs door for a raving woman who for half an hour has been screaming and beating at the entrance. Tense, he listens as she comes stomping up the stairwell, down the hall, panting like a bear, and slams a door. In the middle of the night, often, he wakes to the scream of sirens.

———

QUIETER EVENINGS, WHEN NOT AT WORK on his word processor or reading or writing letters, the young man sits in the light of his single lamp, alone in the chilly room, contemplating for hours the thought-problem of a fly crawling on a billiard table, the relative passage of time for the fly as it crosses that proportional vastness. What is a minute to the fly? What is an inch? The problem mystifies the young man. It has something to do with space itself as a means of experiencing time.

———

IN THE BASEMENT of the Concord Free Public Library, the young man turns the pages of a handwritten manuscript in a thin green binding. It is Thoreau's essay "Walking," written on the author's very deathbed in 1862.

"I'm a part of this history now," the young man will later write in his journal. "It was just a question of pages changing hands in the course of time. Thoreau's life and mine physically intersected in the three hours I spent poring over his handwriting. The pages had come to me for my turn, and my hands received them. I am not cut off. I can realize myself here and everywhere as an invulnerable link in a chain, implicitly tied to all of the ages before me."

———

"WILL NOT MAN GROW to greater perfection intellectually as well as physically under these influences? ... I trust that we shall be more imaginative, that our thoughts will be clearer, fresher, and more ethereal, as our sky, — our understanding more comprehensive and broader, like our plains, — our intellect generally on a grander scale, like our thunder and lightning, our rivers and mountains and forests, — and our hearts shall even correspond in breadth and depth and grandeur to our inland seas."
    —Henry David Thoreau, "Walking"

———

IS THE IMAGINATIVE WRITER'S SENSE of time

fundamentally different than other people's? Does the imaginative writer — whatever his subject or setting — identify more strongly with the centuries than with his own time?

————

"In practical life, time is a form of wealth with which we are stingy. In literature, time is a form of wealth to be spent at leisure and with detachment."
  —Italo Calvino

————

Some days, the young man wanders Boston and Cambridge. He meanders in Harvard Yard, thinking of young Thoreau at college here, how during school holidays Thoreau would commute the fourteen miles between Cambridge and Concord by foot. The young man recalls Emerson's "American Scholar," first delivered as an address at Harvard. Student Thoreau was probably in the audience that day. He would have heard these words: "The scholar is that man who must take up into himself all the ability of the time, all the contributions of the past, all the hopes of the future. He must be a university of knowledges. If there be one lesson more than another which should pierce his ear, it is, The world is nothing, the man is all; in yourself is the law of all nature, and you know not yet how a globule of sap ascends; in yourself slumbers the whole of Reason; it is for you to know all; it is for you to dare all."

Amidst the red brick buildings on Harvard Yard is one marked Emerson Hall. The young man walks right in. There in the corridor is Emerson himself, larger than life in bronze. Enthroned in a large chair, the chair itself elevated on a concrete plinth, he sits Lincoln-like amid the folds of his frock coat, half-smiling. The young man receives his presence like a benediction, then proceeds to wander the building, looking into the empty classrooms. In the dank daylight of one unlit lecture hall the young man stands before the rows of fixed wooden seats, remembering himself, recognizing his foreignness. He will go back to Lowell tonight. His loneliness immaculate, he will sit reading beside his single lamp, deep in the earnest impracticality and muddle of his work. He'll sleep another night on the air mattress on the floor. He'll wake to being lost in his mind for another day. Now the young man turns to the cloudy blackboard. He finds a piece of chalk and, in letters half as large as he is, draws Emerson's own words:

TRUST THYSELF

———

T HE YOUNG MAN WOULD NOT STAY LONG in Lowell. He felt the winter coming and he didn't have a proper coat. One night he carried his belongings down to the basement and abandoned them there beside the washing machines — all but his word processor and books, which would return with him to California. He would grow accustomed, in days and years after, to carrying books everywhere he went. Already he understood that for a writer, books and experience were often interchangeable, that books were lives distilled, and that they were teachers, and that through books he could move freely through time.

———

B OOKS COULD MONUMENTALIZE and commemorate. In London the prior year, he had brought with him W. Jackson Bate's *John Keats* and a Penguin paperback of the selected poetry, as well as an old leather-bound volume, *Poetical Works of Keats*, which he carried on pilgrimage and dedicated on the flyleaf one gloomy autumn day:

> *This book went with me to Keats's house on
> Hampstead Heath in England 10/2/97 and
> was here inscribed while I sat on a bench in the
> Vale of Health, that expansive green where Keats*

once sat himself toward the end of his short life,
and told a close friend he believed he was dying
of a broken heart.

———

IN PARIS, YEARS LATER, as he worked on his second novel, he would have with him a whole suitcase of books brought from home. He understood that literature begets literature.

———

WHEN WE ARE YOUNG we look for ourselves in every story. Later on, being lost in our own lives, we are more willing to give ourselves up to the inviolable landscapes and lost time of other narratives, for we come to understand how other stories may enrich us.

———

"NO MAN LIVES IN THE EXTERNAL TRUTHS, among salts and acids, but in the warm phantasmagoric chamber of his brain, with the painted windows and the storied walls." —R.L. Stevenson

———

A LETTER FROM HIS SISTER, received shortly after his arrival in Massachusetts: "When you got off the train, did you feel like you were still moving?"

Variations on a Beginning

1.

I COULD SAY AT THE OUTSET that my father stood nearly six foot eight. That for most of my boyhood he drove a potato chip truck. That his mother was a school teacher, his father the Chief of Police, that they were members of all the clubs and fraternal societies — the Masons, the Shriners, the Elks, and my favorite (they used ceremonial swords!), the Woodsmen of the World. That they were community figures in Watsonville, California, a small agricultural town on Monterey Bay, founded on a long-lost campsite of the 1769 Portolá Expedition.

They lived in the red house with leaded windows and Victorian turrets on the little lane called Sudden Street. They drank and smoked themselves to death, because that was the way of life for happy, prosperous, vivacious folks in their time. My father always told us children of the hours he passed lying awake in his boyhood room listening to his parents' rattling throats, their wheezing and hacking down the hall, and vowed to himself he would never touch a cigarette.

———

2.

I COULD BEGIN WITH GUNS — and not because
they're unique to my story. The chromium and
plastic six-shooters I wore in holsters on every
errand with my mother. My grandfather's five-pound
"paperweight," which was a massive black pistol
encased in lead. One of several mementoes surviving
from his desk at the station, it was, or so we grandkids
were told, something he'd wrenched from a fugitive's
grip during an altercation and arrest, then had cast in
lead as a souvenir. The .22-guage rifle with which my
father was shot one day in the late 1950s, while playing
with his sister shooting targets at a campground, the
dense black smudge of the bullet forever lodged in his
shin, as he never tired of showing us, and how he would
tell the story: "I came up limping saying 'Mom, I'm
shot, I'm shot, she shot me!' and do you know what
Gramma said? 'Oh, Stephen,' she said, 'stop your
fooling and go play,' and then when she looked and saw
the blood she gasped so deep she almost fainted." My
father, his leg outstretched on the ottoman, his trouser
cuff rolled, parts the bristling black hairs on his shin as
he tells it, and my brother and I lean closer. The other
.22 — or was it the same gun? — that lay across the
rafters in the garage, and how my brother and I got it
down to play with one Saturday afternoon. We were
standing in our driveway, my brother aiming it here

and there and I fumbling with the box of shells, when
our mother (a neighbor having called to alert her) came
out to stop us.

3.

THERE WAS ONCE A MURDER at Heights
Market, a mile from our house. It started with
the deranged man whom Mr. Heights kicked
out of his store for spitting on the produce. The man
returned some hours later, waited patiently in the
checkout line, then shotgunned Mr. Heights point-
blank in the face.

But that's a story I never heard growing up. I learned
it only this year from my father, on a nostalgic drive
through Watsonville.

4.

THERE ARE MANY STARTING POINTS, it seems —
memories and anecdotes shaken loose from
the narrative I or my folk have constructed,
pieces that don't seem to fit in any one place. For
instance, some years ago, my mysterious inability to
wear a watch. How the hands would come loose and
swing about the dial. Three different watches I tried
and, one after the other, returned them all, defective.

Always the hands were fixed when I bought a watch, adrift once I'd worn it a day or so.

This, of course, is not a story but merely something that happened, which is different. And I might tell how this mystery passed, how, eventually, I could wear a watch again (I wear one now), but this is not the same thing as a story's end.

———

ARE WE ROOTED IN STORIES, narratives, anecdotes, or something else? A loose and airy soil. A depository for oddments of all kinds. How do we begin to tell where we came from? The things that shaped us, or seemed to.

5.

I COULD BEGIN WITH NAMES. Of places. Of loved ones. (And must I change the loved ones' names on paper? Well, you've already met my father). So, names.

Allen, my middle name, derives from old Vermont, or so the family story goes — the name is an ancient ligature to that colonial figure (a character in many stories himself) Ethan Allen, of the Green Mountain Boys, the militia whose members were sure they could capture Montreal. As a middle name I share it with my great grandfather Ernest Kurzweil, a skilled gardener who lived to be ninety-six, who fought in the Great War in France (I've inherited his pocket map of Paris), whose life was saved because he knew how to make gravy (and was transferred from common soldier to cook), whose people, in his mother's line, were Wenzel, a family that enjoyed a minor dynasty in Prague where, in the last decades of the nineteenth-century, one of them became related to Rainer Maria Rilke by marriage, something wholly unknown to me until I'd been writing a book about Rilke for years.

Or the name Robley, as the family of my great grandmother Avis was called, and the winding country track outside Monterey — still called Robley Road — in that gorgeous, distinctively Northern California valley known as the Corral de Tierra, which Steinbeck dubbed The Pastures of Heaven in his book of that title.

Or, while I am following the names in this way, I could tell of old Mrs. Rodgers, whose maiden name was Steinbeck, and who was known in Watsonville to be the author's aged sister, and how she lived with her husband in the great white farmhouse on a one-acre plot which was all that remained of the farm, while in the asphalt lot next door (the shopping center called East Lake Village), stood Lambert's Market where my father worked, a long yellow apron draped over his shirt and tie, and a pricing gun always at hand, and how he would carry over, once a week, old Mrs. Rodgers' standing order of groceries and think, *The famous author's sister, how 'bout that.*

    I could then mention, again, that recent nostalgic drive with my father through town, and how we found the old farm lot empty, a barren scrubland of weeds, and the grand white house gone, torn down for reasons we couldn't know.*

6.

THE ORDER OF EVENTS, I've long believed, is not so important. The truth is much larger than chronology, and sequence alone, convincing as it may be, can serve to explain in only the most specious way. Because the truth is (isn't it?) that so little can stand on explanation. What joins our days together into a lived experience is not the linear, calendric, forward march of hours, months, years, and epochs which, for the sake of civilization, orders time for us by our consent. What joins our days together into a lived experience is, more truthfully, a vague webwork, a gossamer of associations, memories, and sensations. However much we claim to believe in a standardized chronology of event, this gossamer remains central to who and what we are. Manifesting the insubstantial evidence of our lives, it permits very little elaboration or embellishment from the rational

---

* In fact the house was relocated to the county fairgrounds.

linear world. Adhering to the skeleton of memory, it catches everything — or everything important — storing impressions we rarely understand at first, but like a language as one learns it these impressions accrete meaning over time.

"When you write," said Edmond Jabès, "you do not know whether you are obeying the moment or eternity." Isn't that also a description of what it's like to be alive, to possess consciousness and memory?

"In practical life, time is a form of wealth with which we are stingy," said Italo Calvino. "In literature, time is a form of wealth to be spent at leisure and with detachment."

And yet there's the rigid demand placed on writers today: that they "sell" their stories to the reader, beginning with Page One and continuing with every page thereafter. Always a forward march. I'm not unaware of this demand. But oh, the perverseness: expecting little from the writer beyond manipulation, little from the reader beyond passivity.

Dear Reader, How about this: I sell you nothing (selling is the bookstore's business). What you read here is freely given: my consciousness to yours. And may your reading be something like the Zen experience Master Shunryu Suzuki-Roshi describes: "It is not like going out in a shower in which you know when you get wet. In a fog, you do not know you are getting wet, but as you keep walking you get wet little by little."

7.

BUT *NARRATIVE,* WHICH I DO BELIEVE IN, what is that and where does it fit when one seeks to retell a thing from its beginning?

To narrate: from the Latin *narratus,* which is the plural of *narrare,* and stems from *gnarus,* or knowing, and relates to *gnoscere* or *noscere,* to know. So sayeth Webster's Ninth, which by that definition is itself a *narrative* compendium, for *to know* the meaning of words as its pages do is a form of narration.

And down from my shelf comes a *Glossary of Literary Terms* to say: "A narrative is a story, whether told in prose or verse, involving events, characters, and what the characters say and do." And then adds this, the best part: "It should be noted that there is an implicit narrative element even in many *lyric* poems."

One knows something, then, or comes to know something, and tells the story of coming to know it, or, *in telling the story comes to know it.* Shades upon shades, but none of them, let us note, associated with selling. No, for to know, to come to know, and to tell one's way into knowing — these are not of the order of merchandise but of gift.

———

8.

IN A SIXTH-CENTURY COURTYARD in Milan a man hears a disembodied child's voice imploring him to take up the scriptures and read. Obeying, the man's eyes fall upon some words of Saint Paul and immediately "the light of confidence" floods his heart. He hurries inside his house to tell his mother he's been saved. This is Saint Augustine's moment of conversion as he himself describes it. In a single profound instant he awakens to his place in a larger story as told by Paul. His bright surge of spiritual "confidence" is the form of knowing peculiar to narrative. He has awakened to narrative's power — to narrative as a way of recognizing where one belongs, where one is rooted, narrative as a voice whose sole interest is discovery, *coming to know*, narrative as *voice*, which one may willingly follow.

9.

I'VE LONG LOVED THE BIBLICAL STORY of Samuel, which is about hearing a voice, about listening and coming to know:

> Samuel was lying down in the temple of the Lord, where the ark of God was. Then the

Lord called "Samuel! Samuel!" and he said,
"Here I am!" and ran to Eli, and said, "Here I
am, for you called me." But Eli said, "I did not
call, my son; lie down again." So he went and
lay down. The Lord called again, "Samuel!"
Samuel got up and went to Eli and said,
"Here I am, for you called me." But Eli said, "I
did not call, my son; lie down again." Now
Samuel did not yet know the Lord, and the
word of the Lord had not yet been revealed to
him. The Lord called Samuel again, a third
time. And he got up and went to Eli and said,
"Here I am, for you called me." Then Eli
perceived that the Lord was calling the boy.
Therefore Eli said to Samuel, "Go, lie down;
and if he calls you, you shall say, 'Speak, Lord,
for your servant is listening.'" So Samuel
went and lay down in his place. Now the Lord
came and stood there, calling as before,
"Samuel! Samuel!" And Samuel said, "Speak,
for your servant is listening."

I could start, then, with Samuel, and how I first
learned his story late one night when I was nine or ten
years old and heard, in the dark of my boyhood
bedroom, a voice of my own, a voice so clear and
voluble that it stirred me from my near-sleep, and how
this voice frightened me enough that I got up and
walked down the hall to stand by my parents' bed in
the dark, to wake my mother and tell her about the

voice, and how she asked me what the voice had said
and I told her it had said, "You're going to die," and
how, after a soft sympathetic noise, my mother, still
lying beside my sleeping father in their bed, told me
the story of Samuel, and how I loved that story
immediately and yet couldn't help saying, "But what if
it wasn't God this time?" and how my mother told me I
should pray about it and then I would not be afraid.

So again in the night, as it was for my father in his
youth, the child's thoughts led to the parents' bed.

So, as it was for Samuel, the act of discovery is a
sleepwalk. The boy rises from bed to walk in the dark,
to hear a story, to pray. And isn't prayer itself a
sleepwalk? And isn't reading a sleepwalk also, much as
writing always is for the writer?

That night I went and lay down in my place, but a
story had begun. Already, praying myself back to sleep,
I was telling myself the story.

Aren't our roots a kind of sleep whose dream we are?

Essential to Samuel's story is his aloneness before
God. Only in the aloneness of his sleep could Samuel
hear the voice and know it for the fateful thing it was.

Dear Reader, go slowly, at your leisure.

———

10.

I N THAT OLD KOAN ABOUT THE TREE that falls in
the unpeopled forest and does it make a sound, we
have the antecedent for the confused koan of our
hyperconnected contemporary moment, which goes: *If I
am alone, do I exist?*

Dear Reader, are you asking this, as you think about
your own beginnings — as such thoughts reflect to you
the passage of time, your irreversible status as guest in
a neverending stream of person and event?

11.

T HE YEAR I STARTED MIDDLE SCHOOL, my
mother redid the wallpaper in our house, and
behind the old paper in two places — the
stairs landing and the master bathroom — she
discovered large portraits drawn in charcoal. Both were
very finely done, each spookily vivid with personality.
For almost a week she left them exposed, and how
indelibly I remember the one on the landing, and how I
sat on the stairs before it, spellbound. It was the full-
body portrait of a man in uniform, a soldier. The
portrait was taller than my father, nine feet in length at
least, and though the soldier merely stood there, arms

at his sides and boots together, and though his face staring out at me was mostly expressionless, his colossal stature alone lent him a vaguely threatening quality.

I couldn't identify the soldier's uniform then, though remembering it today I see that it was plainly German and dated from World War One. He wore a spiked helmet (a Pickelhaube) and side-whiskers, his chin neatly shaved. Adorning the stiff collar at his throat was an iron cross, black straps intersected diagonally across his chest, and his breeches were snugly tucked into knee-high black boots.

For the near-week that my mother left the drawing exposed on our wall, I stared into the figure's smudged charcoal eyes. Why was this soldier there? When, if ever, would he see the light again, after my mother put the new wallpaper up? Once covered over, wouldn't he still be there, always? How could our house be anything but animate after this?

12.

HOW BEAUTIFUL AND ALIVE A SECRET CAN BE, and what secrets there are in the layers of things.

"If a secret cannot be maintained, we are in a totalitarian space," said Jacques Derrida.

Is the *knowing* in narrative a surrendering of all secrets? I don't think so, though we're often led to believe this. Let us agree that there are many ways to tell our stories. And yet, isn't every story a form of secrecy?

―――

All you have to know is whether you're lying, or whether you're trying to tell the truth, you can't afford to make a mistake about that distinction any longer.
   —John Berger

―――

O nce, in Saint Paul's Cathedral, I heard a voice speaking a prayer that went like this: *Lord God, make us humble. Unweave our thoughts, uncomplicate our hearts, that we might lay down our books and step into the dark. Make us empty with longing, that we will seek you.*

―――

S ome days while sitting and working you merely catch the hem of a thing. And that is a lot. It's a lot.

―――

And in the astonishment that comes, sometimes, of reading, is it not largely a book's having been *finished* by its writer that astonishes us? That too is a lot. Perhaps it is what matters most of all.

13.

DEAR READER, with the steady searching turn of the pages our time goes slow.

14.

RAINER MARIA RILKE, WHOSE MOTHER, when he was a child, encouraged him in the belief that the remains of a young revolutionary were interred in the parlor wall of the family's Prague apartment — Rilke, in later life, would painstakingly recopy a letter he was writing rather than tolerate the defacing of his gorgeous calligraphy by an ink blemish or compositional mistake.

He wrote some eleven thousand letters this way. It wasn't idle fussiness — it was the work of a poet. "Mon Maître," he wrote to Auguste Rodin on September 11, 1902, "It is not only to do a study that I have come to you, — it was in order to ask you: how must one live? And you have replied: by working. And this I understand well. I see that to work is to live without dying."

15.

It is to be noted (Mrs. William James reported) that even after Henry James lapsed into a coma, his hands continued to move across the bedsheet as if he were writing.

—*The Complete Notebooks of Henry James*, pg. 582

I F TO NARRATE IS TO KNOW, then writing is always an act of searching, of seeking out what lies at the bottom of things, the roots and foundations. To write is to take root.

———

T urning back to the dark hall, the boy of nine or ten went and lay down in his place.

———

Dear Reader, the story uncoils and coils again and again.

You've heard this one before. You know it already. Still you say it over once more. Still you listen for the new inflection.

The story is never not beginning.

Notes & Acknowledgments

For their receptivity and early support for portions of this work, I'm grateful to the following:

Robert Antoni, Jeff Baker and *The Oregonian* Books section of 2010-2015, Kathleen Holt and Oregon Humanities Magazine, *Pilgrimage* magazine, Thea Prieto and *Portland Review*, Dan DeWeese and *Propeller Quarterly*, the erstwhile editors of defunct *Tin House* magazine, Pam Wells and Peter Field and *The Timberline Review*.

Thank you to Dr. Micah Sadigh for his inspiring Vienna Lectures in the summer of 2015. Gratitude to Dr. Connor McNamara and Catriona Crowe for their compelling talks at Dublin's Trinity College and aboard the bus, to Dan/Thomas Small for the conversation on Yeats, to Christine Gerchow for providing the occasion to gather my thoughts, and to the late John Berger and the late Ihab Hassan for generosity and immeasurable encouragements.

This book is funded in part by the Regional Arts & Culture Council.

Excerpts from the diary of Miguel Costansó derive from *The Discovery of San Francisco Bay: The Portolá*

Expedition of 1769-1770: The Diary of Miguel Costansó, edited by Peter Browning.

The statement "It is the nature of music to be ongoing" originates in *The Unanswered Question: Six Talks at Harvard* by Leonard Bernstein.

INDEX

www.ingramcontent.com/pod-product-compliance
Lightning Source LLC
Chambersburg PA
CBHW030630020726
47493CB00006B/1643